THE
INHERITANCE
OF A DREAM

THE INHERITANCE OF A DREAM

The Memoirs of Dr. Irene H. Brodie

A NATIONALLY-ESTEEMED EDUCATOR, PHILANTHROPIST, and PUBLIC OFFICIAL

Irene H. Brodie, Ed.D

WITH

Vincent Williams

Published by Pollster Media Group, Inc.
Chicago, Illinois USA

Pollster Media Group, Inc. First Edition, January 2015

Published in the United States of America by Pollster Media Group, Inc., Chicago, Illinois

Pollster Media Group, Inc.
150 North Michigan Ave., Suite 2800
Chicago, IL 60601

www.PollsterMediaGroup.com

Printed in the United States of America

Library of Congress Cataloguing-in-Publication Data

Brodie, Irene H., 1931–, Williams, Vincent 1965–
The Inheritance of a Dream: The Memoirs of Dr. Irene H. Brodie/
Irene H. Brodie, Ed.D with Vincent Williams. — 1st ed.

p. cm.
Includes bibliographical references and index.
ISBN-13: 978-0-615-87212-4 (Hardcover)

Cover portrait by Carey Muhammad
Interior design and layout by Eric Cimino
Authors' photo (back cover) by Kenneth Wright
All photos, unless otherwise credited, are provided courtesy of Dr. Irene H. Brodie.

"The Negro has been here in America since 1619...He is not going anywhere else; this country is his home. He wants to do his part to help make his city, state, and nation a better place for everyone, regardless of color and race."

—*Medgar W. Evers*
Civil Rights Leader

CONTENTS

CONTENTS

DEDICATION

While reflecting on my life, my numerous challenges and my achievements, I would not have been able to attain the academic, spiritual, and personal success without the love, support, and guidance from my dearly departed parents, Ira Edwin Hale and Ressie Alice Hale. They instilled in my siblings and me the value of a good, quality education and the need to develop a good work ethic. These values that were instilled in me as a little girl have served as a guiding light, allowing me to mature into the woman I am today. Mother and Father, I love you, and I will always be thankful for the values I was taught.

I had passed on these same values to my daughter, my only child, Jeraye, whose life was tragically cut short by a painful illness. Jeraye had such a zest for life and a passion for people that not even her declining health could diminish. In fact, her aspirations to help those less fortunate inspired me. It is from this spirit that I found strength and acquired my great passion for public service. I inherited Jeraye's dream.

†

ACKNOWLEDGMENTS

I am honored to take the time and give thanks to a host of family, friends, staff, students, neighbors, local area business owners, supporters, and well-wishers, many of whom my achievements and my success would not have been possible without. I must thank Tyrone Haymore, president of the Robbins Historical Society & Museum, and former Robbins village clerk and member of the Village Board of Trustees. Mr. Haymore has helped to provide a tremendous amount of assistance with historical data that has helped make this book most accurate and informative. I thank you for your cooperation, generosity, and tireless effort in this regard, and I wish the absolute best to the Robbins History Museum on its future endeavors and growth, especially as it celebrates and chronicles the Village of Robbins' 100th Anniversary as an incorporated municipality on December 14, 2017!

I thank all the staff and municipal employees of the Village of Robbins for their remarkable dedication and loyal support over the many years that I've had the honor of serving as mayor and village clerk. Thank you! Napoleon Haney, former village administrator, thank you. You reflect the best talent in public administration, and the people of Robbins have certainly benefitted from your hard work and commitment to make Robbins a better place for its residents to live. Thank you for making my latter years in the office of mayor as smooth as possible as I faced many challenges, personal and professional, as I officially transitioned into retirement. I expect that you will have a great future ahead of yourself in public service, young man. I am also grateful to the late Beverly Gavin, who preceded Napoleon Haney as village administrator. Together, we achieved some really great things for the people of Robbins. I expect our accomplishments and efforts will endure for many years to come.

I must thank everyone who served in my administration as mayor at the Robbins Village Hall—every employee of every department, buildings, police and fire, public works, water and administration. Working together during my six consecutive terms as mayor, we implemented changes in various departments that resulted in the efficiency of operations and accountability by department heads and their employees. The people of Robbins will always be indebted to you for your hard work. A special thanks to Buildings Department secretary, Vielka Sterling whose bright smile and kindness so often radiated the entire

ACKNOWLEDGMENTS

Village Hall. Thank you Sherry Thomas, our office manager and Lyniece Toliver, Water Department clerk for all of the hard work you have done.

Lillian Crockling, my executive secretary, thank you for helping to keep me organized and on schedule for what was often a very busy and hectic pace at the office. I am very appreciative to have had you working alongside me for the past several years. I wish you the very best.

Thank you to Sharon McNeal, Vincent Williams, Joshua Coblentz, and Jacqueline Mathews for the countless hours that you devoted to help bring this project to fruition. Your unwavering dedication, commitment, and support is greatly appreciated. Thank you Darrell L. Booker, Jr. for your assistance with research, and inspiring thoughts, constant support and encouragement that kept us motivated and helped us to make it across the finish line.

And last but not least, a very heart-felt thank you to my co-author and publishing executive, Vincent Williams. Thank you for your relentless effort in seeing this project through from conception to completion. You and your team at Pollster Media Group have greatly assisted me in reaching a personal goal spanning over at least two decades, writing and publishing my biography and memoirs. Thank you very much for helping me with bringing my literary work to fruition.

Dr. Irene H. Brodie
November 2014

PROLOGUE

CIVIL RIGHTS AND QUALITY EDUCATION

*"A child born to a Black mother in a state like Mississippi…
has exactly the same rights as a white baby born to the
wealthiest person in the United States. It's not true, but I
challenge anyone to say it is not a goal worth working for."*

— Thurgood Marshall
Former Associate Justice of the
United States Supreme Court

Ira and Ressie Hale, parents of Irene Hale, lived in the midst of the Jim Crow Era. They were subjected to poll taxes and literacy tests as a precondition for voting. Women in the United States were not afforded full voting rights until 1920, right around the time Ressie had come of age. In the South, racial segregation in public places, including educational facilities, was the law. Jim Crow laws in practice, led to conditions for African-Americans that were inferior to those provided for white Americans, and institutionalized a number of economic, educational and social disadvantages. Given the tumultuous political and social environment of their time, Irene's parents could not have envisioned the political feats that their daughter would attain in the future.

In the United States, up until the mid-1960s, a poll tax was used as a precondition for the ability to vote, instituted primarily for African-Americans. This tax emerged in some states, particularly southern states, in the late nineteenth century as part of the Jim Crow doctrine. After the ability to vote had been extended to all races by the enactment of the Fifteenth Amendment, many southern states enacted poll tax laws as a means of restricting eligible African-American voters. These laws, along with unfairly implemented literacy tests and extra-legal intimidation, achieved the desired effect of disenfranchising African-American and Native-American voters.

In 1937, the United States Supreme Court took up this matter in the case of *Breedlove v. Suttles,* and ruled that the poll tax was constitutional. Resulting from a political compromise and ratified in 1964, the Twenty-Fourth Amendment abolished the use of the poll tax or any other tax as a precondition for voting in federal elections, but failed to outlaw poll taxes in state elections. Finally, in 1966, in the case of *Harper v. Virginia Board of Elections,* the United States Supreme Court overruled its prior decision in *Breedlove v. Suttles* and extended the prohibition of poll taxes to state elections. The U.S. Supreme Court declared that the imposition of a poll tax in state elections violated the Equal Protection Clause of the Fourteenth Amendment in the United States Constitution.

Growing up in Arkansas and Missouri during the 1940s, Irene Hale attended all-black schools. Segregation was the law of the land under the doctrine of Jim Crow. The years of the 1950s and 1960s represented a period of time in the United States that was marked by social upheaval, civil disobedience, and unrest. Across the South, civil rights demonstrations, boycotts, protests, and sit-ins were occurring. African-Americans had engaged the white power structure, which included local, state, and national governments, in a fight for civil rights, particularly the right to vote and the right to a quality education for African-Americans.

In Mississippi, friends of Irene, James Charles Evers and his younger brother, civil rights leader Medgar Wiley Evers, were aggressively engaged in efforts to overturn segregation at the University of Mississippi. Medgar Evers was named the NAACP's first field secretary. In this position, he helped organize boycotts and set up local chapters of the NAACP. Medgar Evers grew in prominence as a black leader when he launched a multitude of public investigations into the civil rights violations of blacks, including, and most notably, the brutal murder of Emmett Till. Emmett Till was a fourteen year-old black boy from Chicago who was viciously murdered by whites on August 28, 1955 for allegedly whistling at a white woman while visiting relatives in Money, Mississippi. Till's murder drew worldwide attention and was a pivotal event that caused a spark that ignited the Civil Rights Movement in the United States.

African-American attorney and future United States Supreme Court Justice

Thurgood Marshall led the fight to dismantle the "separate but equal" doctrine in public education. Marshall argued that school segregation was a violation of individual rights under the Fourteenth Amendment. He also asserted that the only reason for continuing to have separate schools for whites and blacks was to keep people who were slaves "as near to that stage as possible."

In 1954, in the case of *Brown v. Board of Education,* the Supreme Court declared state laws establishing separate public schools for black and white students unconstitutional. The decision overturned the *Plessy v. Ferguson* decision of 1896, which allowed state sponsored segregation as it applied to public education. On May 17, 1954, the Supreme Court decision declared, "separate educational facilities are inherently unequal." The previous decision handed down by the U.S. District Court of Kansas which had previously issued a ruling in favor of public school segregation was reversed.

It was not until after Irene reached adulthood that she would be able to set foot inside a classroom occupied by white students. Even the most optimistic of minds would never have dreamt of the accomplishments and feats that the future would hold for Irene in the field of education.

During the height of the Civil Rights Movement in the United States, the early 1950s through the late 1960s, the South was not the only part of the country that was segregated and where civil rights were being fought for. While segregation in the Southern United States was mandated by law (de jure), in the Northern United States, segregation was generally de facto, not necessarily ordained by law, but rather enacted by practice. The fight for civil rights and to end segregation was pervasive in the North as well. Blatant practices of inequality in Chicago had captured the attention of Dr. Martin Luther King, Jr., and the Civil Rights Movement. Inequality in housing and jobs in the public sector were the prime issues of civil rights activists, in addition to adherents of equal rights to quality education for black children. Chicago Public Schools were very much segregated. There was serious overcrowding in the classrooms of woefully deteriorating black schools, while modernized white schools were operating with an increasing number of empty classrooms. Rather than allow black students to occupy the empty rooms in white schools, mobile classes were established by bringing in trailers and converting old buildings and warehouses into schools. Under the leadership of Chicago Mayor Richard J. Daley and Chicago Public Schools Superintendent Benjamin Willis, this was a way of sidestepping the demand for integration. In 1964 school boycotts were organized and tens of thousands of black children were kept home in protest of the poor and inhumane conditions that they were subjected to at black schools.

In 1964, a small riot broke out in the predominantly black community of Dixmoor, Illinois, a neighboring community of Robbins, Illinois, also a majority black and mixed-race suburb located about 15 miles southwest of Chicago. This rioting occurred during a summer of extreme racial unrest across America. Dixmoor gained notice due to a one-day riot that involved over one thousand persons with local and state police. The riot became known as the "Gin Bottle Riot." This event was unsuspected because Dixmoor was a pleasant ranch-house style suburb that, prior to this racial outbreak of violence, had taken well to integration. The eruption of the riot resulted from a black woman being arrested for allegedly attempting to steal a pint of gin and claiming that she had been roughed up by a Dixmoor liquor store owner, Michael "Big Mike" LaPota, a white, fifty-two year-old, 265-pound ex-offender. Soon the allegation spread through Dixmoor and into the neighboring City of Harvey. Soon afterwards, a crowd gathered in a parking lot across from the liquor store, and one of the participants threw a rock through the store's window. Looting and theft ensued. Dixmoor's small police force of ten immediately called for help, and was joined by a reinforcement of state police. State and local officials were bombarded with rocks, and for several hours they used tear gas and high-pressured fire hoses to force back the mob.

The riot erupted again for a second day when rioters propelled Molotov cocktails onto the rooftop of LaPota's liquor store, setting it ablaze. In all, over fifty people were injured during the rioting and over seventy blacks and whites were arrested. This event dashed Dixmoor's long history of amicable race relations. Integration in Dixmoor began in the 1960s, and by 1990, thirty years later, fifty-eight percent of the community's population was African-American, a ratio that held steady until the year 2000.

Even after Irene married J.E. Brodie and they moved to the Chicago area from Missouri, they had not imagined that the struggle for civil rights and quality education for African-Americans in Chicago would be just as prevalent and as equally intense as what they had witnessed and experienced in the South and in Missouri.

†

1

MY FAMILY'S JOURNEY

"It was an enjoyable time to be alive, and to be in the clean, fresh air and having vegetables that were plentiful and farm animals that you raised for food. There was plenty of food. We had so much we didn't realize there was such a thing as people who didn't have."

— *Dr. Irene H. Brodie*

Irene Hale was born February 27, 1931 in Armorel, Arkansas, a small, largely rural, unincorporated community with a population of about 350, located in Mississippi County, just outside of Blytheville, Arkansas. Ira Edwin Hale and his wife, Ressie Alice Elder were Irene's proud parents. They met in Tennessee and moved to Arkansas in search of a better life together. Ressie Alice Elder was born August 13, 1902 in Ripley, Tennessee and was the seventh child of eight daughters born to John Elder and Celia Moody-Elder. Ira Edwin Hale was born March 31, 1886 to Ted Hale and Mattie Barnett-Hale. Ira had a younger sibling, Lerla Mae Cole, who was born June 2, 1891. Ira Edwin Hale and Ressie Alice Elder joined in matrimony in Charleston, Missouri. To this union, six children were born, Ethel Mae, Evelyn, Irene, Bertha, Ira Jr., and Leo.

Ira had encountered conflict in his hometown in Tennessee when he stood up as a small businessman against discrimination aimed at him by white business owners who wanted to deny him fair compensation for produce that was grown on his farm. During the early 1900s in the South, blacks were often the victims of discrimination, particularly blacks like Ira, who owned their own businesses, and got paid a lesser value for their farm-raised produce than their white counterparts. In many cases, white business owners would offer to pay substantially less than the going rate, for produce being farmed and sold by blacks in the South. In some cases, whites would attempt to defraud black farmers out of their produce altogether. One tactic that was regularly employed by discriminating whites was to offer to buy produce, take possession of the produce, and then outright refuse to pay black farmers for their goods. This tactic caused many black farmers in the South to go out of business. However, Mr. Hale would stand his ground and demand fair value for his produce. This would sometimes spark confrontations with angry whites who were determined to maintain discriminatory practices toward blacks in the Jim Crow South. On one occasion, tensions had risen so high between Ira and a white man that Ira had no choice but to leave the State of Tennessee and relocate his family to Arkansas in an effort to assure the safety of him and his family.

Ira and Ressie had a strong love for each other and were both deeply rooted in their faith. Ira was raised as a Protestant and Ressie was raised as a Baptist. Their deep faith and strong determination would help them endure many obstacles as they worked to successfully build their business as sharecroppers.

After living in Arkansas, Ira then purchased a small farm in Poplar Bluff, Missouri. Following that, Mr. and Mrs. Hale decided it was time to begin to grow their family. The Hale daughters became a blossoming part of the Hale Family, and they would all be raised to work on the farm. Ira and Ressie would also welcome two sons to their family. In fact, their first child was a boy named Ira E. Hale, Jr. or "I-E." Sadly, he died at birth of pleurisy. Pleurisy, also known as pleuritis, is an inflammation of the pleura, the lining of the lung's membrane cavity. Years later, Ressie also later gave birth to another boy, Leo Hale, who, after a few years of battling the same illness would also have his life cut short. Irene had grown close to her younger brother Leo, and she adored him. Although his life was cut short at the age of three, the years that he spent with Irene and the rest of the family were precious, and provided a lifetime of memories for the entire Hale Family.

While Ira Hale would often encourage his daughters to excel academically and prepare for college, it was Mrs. Hale who would often play the role of disciplinarian when any of the girls did not behave, perform, or conduct themselves in a lady-like fashion. Mrs. Hale did not hesitate to break a twig off of one of the farm trees for use as a switch in order to let the girls know she meant business.

On the farm, the family raised livestock to sell to butchers, meat processors, and other commercial establishments, as well as for their own personal consumption. Chickens, cattle, and hogs were the most popular livestock raised on the farm. They raised chickens in significant quantity, as they were a family favorite served at the dinner table, and a regular source of fresh eggs. The cows provided a source for fresh milk and butter. It was part of the Hale girls' daily routine to squeeze fresh, sweet milk from the family's herd of cows. On the farm, the family grew a wide variety of vegetables and spices including corn, greens, beans, beets, and peppers. They grew cantaloupes and watermelons, and they also harvested walnuts from the farm's walnut trees. The farm was complete with machinery for plowing the fields, and the family owned a horse-drawn wagon. Like typical farmers, the Hales awakened to begin their day at the crack of dawn, and worked long hours, often until sunset, in order to make each day a productive, and profitable one for the family farm.

Life on the farm brought with it all of the freedom and joys that one would imagine comes from owning and working on a productive farm. Fresh, homegrown food was in abundance. Ressie enjoyed cooking for her family and she took great pride in teaching Ethel, Evelyn, and Irene how to prepare meals as well. Fresh, homegrown greens topped with sweet Southern Cha Cha were a regular favorite served for dinner. Greens were one of Irene's favorite foods. The sound of a chicken's cry while being butchered, followed by being seasoned and placed in the fryer was a sound that everyone in the Hale Family had grown accustomed to, prior to selecting from a full platter, their choice of select pieces of Ressie's fresh, farm-raised, golden fried chicken. Fresh, buttery fried corn, greens, candied yams, and hot-water cornbread would provide a hearty and memorable meal for the entire family. On special occasions, Ressie would prepare wild duck, rabbit, or squirrel with rice and homegrown string beans. Mrs. Hale also taught the children how to ground and process fresh sausage from their pork and beef stock. The livestock and the fresh produce grown on the Hale Farm made for the freshest food that could be found almost anywhere in the country.

Ressie taught the girls how to preserve their farm-raised produce as well. They would pick and clean, farm-grown greens, cook them, and then pack them in mason jars to preserve for another day. Oftentimes, they would freeze and preserve an abundance of food during the farm's high yielding summer season, so that they would have plenty to eat during the cold, winter months. Ressie and the girls would also cook and preserve peaches and other fruits for use in homemade jellies and pastries. Fresh, farm-raised cucumbers were made into tasty pickles and preserved in mason jars, and so were Irene's personal favorite, pickled beets. Growing up on the farm, Irene cherished eating pickled beets. She became such a connoisseur of pickled beets that her sister, Evelyn, nicknamed her "Beetie." When Ressie Hale was not busy helping to tend to the farm, cooking, and looking after the children, she enjoyed knitting comforters and quilts for family and friends.

Ira worked as a veterinarian. He became so good at keeping livestock healthy that he gained a reputation for being one of the best and most sought out veterinarians in the area. Some of the largest farm owners and raisers of livestock depended on Ira to help them maintain a healthy herd of cattle, pigs, and other livestock. It was often said by local farmers that if Ira couldn't cure a cow of its ailments, it was destined to die.

Having cut short his formal education in order to raise and support his family, Ira was largely self-educated. He successfully practiced as a veterinarian, performing comparably better than some of his college-educated counterparts in town. Ira learned all too well the benefit of attending college and the opportunities that would become available as a result of a good education accompanied by an attained college degree. Even though Ira was among the most respected practicing veterinarians in the community, he often felt that some opportunities were denied him in favor of some of his less capable veterinarian counterparts, simply because they possessed college degrees. This was, in part, one of the reasons he implored his daughters to realize the importance of pursuing a college education.

Ira and Ressie were levied a poll tax in order to exercise their desire to vote in elections. During this time in American history, in the Jim Crow South, blacks were forced to pay a tax, or made to pass reading tests as a way to deter them from participating in the election process. This was another reason Ira wanted his daughters to become college educated.

Owning and operating the family farm proved to be an ideal way to raise a family for the Hales. It also proved to be an excellent way of instilling discipline in the children. Since all the Hale children were assigned their various chores to help operate and maintain the farm, they learned at a very early age the importance of dedication and hard work. Whether it was milking the cows, plucking the chickens, or picking cotton, the Hale children realized that prosperity only came as a result of relentless dedication and hard work. They would instill these basic principles within themselves and apply them to life's future challenges.

Irene was able to hold her own in terms of working on the farm, and she had by far outperformed the expectations of others with her ability to pick cotton. On average, Irene picked 180 pounds of cotton per day, which was considered exceptional, especially during days of hot, inclement weather. Many wondered how she was able to reach that level of productivity. Her strong character and work ethic showed early in her life.

†

2

THE HALE GIRLS

"My father strongly encouraged us all to go to college. He'd often say, 'In case you don't find a good enough man to marry, a good college education will enable you to take care of yourself.'"

— Dr. Irene H. Brodie

Irene Hale excelled as an honors student. Her high level of academic achievement in school led her to accelerate grade levels at an early age. By the time Irene reached age sixteen, she was on her way to college. She continued to excel, and soon earned her bachelor's degree. As a matter of fact, all four of the Hale sisters would go on to attend college, and all of them would major in education and become teachers.

Ethel Mae Hale was the eldest sister. Evelyn was the second eldest, followed by Irene and Bertha, the youngest sister. Since they all enjoyed school and achieved academic success, some of their teachers took notice and began to refer to the Hale sisters as the "Hale Girls." Bertha, being the youngest of the clan, would often find herself compared to one of her elder sisters by a teacher who remembered having taught one of them. Fortunately for Bertha, her elder sisters all performed well and prospered with their academic coursework, so they provided a good model for Bertha to pattern herself after.

As a teenager, Irene earned a reputation for being fearless and tough when she demonstrated to some of the neighborhood bullies that she was not afraid to use her hands to defend herself or her sisters. There were times when Irene would have to stand up and fight for her elder sister, Evelyn. One neighborhood girl would often attempt to bully Evelyn after school. Evelyn refused to stand up to the girl and, as a result, the bullying intensified. Things came to a head one day when Irene found out about the bullying and decided to forego her normal walk home with friends, and instead took a different path with Evelyn. On this particular day, it seemed that a larger than normal group of girls began to follow Irene and Evelyn in anticipation of a confrontation with the bullying girl. Sure enough, just as the girls made their way down the road and out of the sight of school teachers and staff, a big, robust, and intimidating girl cut Evelyn off at the path and said, "You think you're bad now because you got your sister with you?" Before Evelyn could respond, Irene interceded and said to the girl, "Why don't you leave her alone? She's not bothering you." "I'm not talking to you!" the girl shouted back, while swinging her clenched fist at Irene. Irene blocked her swing and pushed her to the ground. As the girl tried to get up, recovering from her fall, Irene continued to swing, repeatedly hitting her and knocking her to the ground once again. Suddenly, to the amazement of the crowd, the girl began to cry as she stood up and quickly ran away. That bully never bothered Evelyn again.

Although Evelyn was a few years older than Irene, Irene's stellar academic performance accelerated her to the same grade level as Evelyn. Teachers of the two sisters regularly applauded Irene's academic performance. Occasionally, this caused a little animosity and friction between the sisters. At times, Evelyn was jealous of Irene's academic performance and the praise that she regularly received from their teachers.

Ira Hale always encouraged his daughters to go to college and get the best education possible. He often told them that they must have a good education so that in the event they were unable to find a responsible and loving man, their education would afford them independence and the ability to take care of themselves.

All of the Hale Girls began their college studies at Lincoln University, an African-American college located close to the family farm in nearby Jefferson City, Missouri.

Bertha Lee Hale, the youngest sister, attained her bachelor's degree in elementary education from the university. It was also at Lincoln University that Bertha would meet fellow student, George Buckner, who studied industrial art. Within a short time after courting, George and Bertha married.

Bertha went on to attend Central Missouri State University, where she earned her master's degree in education. With degrees in hand, she obtained a position as a teacher at Grey Ridge Elementary School in Grey Ridge, Missouri, where she initially taught first grade students. After a few years, she accepted the position of elementary teacher with the public school system in Kansas City, Missouri, and taught for over thirty years before retiring.

One day while attending college, Evelyn Hale, the second eldest daughter, was walking home, carrying groceries, when she pinched a nerve, sustaining injury that caused her to be hospitalized for an extended period of time. As a result of her injury, she sustained nerve damage that ultimately escalated to other medical issues. As a result, Evelyn had to place her college coursework on hold for several years. Once she fully recuperated, she re-enrolled and earned her bachelor's degree.

Evelyn went on to study at Webster College in Webster Grove, Missouri, a suburb of St. Louis. While in attendance at Webster College, she made significant progress toward earning a master's degree. Evelyn taught elementary students for a while, and then in 1968, she moved to St. Louis, Missouri, where she taught as a reading specialist for the St. Louis Public School System. In 1982, Evelyn relocated to the Washington, D.C. area, where she studied at Howard University, a historically black college. It was at Howard University that Evelyn earned her master and doctorate degrees in divinity. Although Evelyn spent most of her years teaching in the State of Missouri, and more specifically in the inner city schools of St. Louis, she also taught in other parts of the United States, such as Rockville, Maryland. It was in Rockville where she was recognized for her success as a reading teacher. She was awarded Teacher of the Year Award in her very first year as a teacher there. Evelyn pledged and became a member of the Alpha Kappa Alpha sorority, as did her younger sister, Bertha. Irene never joined a sorority, as she spent a lesser amount of time on social activities, instead focusing most of her time on academics. Irene became a member of Kappa Delta Pi, an honors society, and was recognized by various sororities for helping her classmates and other students excel academically.

Ethel Mae Hale, the eldest sister, fell in love with and married Zell Banks of Bell City, Missouri. Shortly after becoming Mrs. Ethel Mae Banks, Ethel transferred to Wayne State University in Detroit, Michigan, where she completed her coursework and earned a bachelor's degree in education. Ethel became a teacher in the Detroit Public Schools. However, prior to relocating to Michigan, she taught for a brief period of time in Missouri. Ethel and Zell were avid boaters. They owned two boats, a cabin cruiser, and a speedboat. They loved fishing, and living in Detroit afforded them immediate access to the Great Lakes.

On March 5, 1962, Ira Edwin Hale, the patriarch of the Hale Family, died of a stroke at the age of seventy-six.

THE INHERITANCE OF A DREAM

Ressie Hale was baptized early in her life, and spent much of her time working in the church until she became disabled. She passed away on January 4, 1978 in Detroit, Michigan, while residing with her eldest daughter, Ethel. Shortly after Ressie's death, Ethel passed away and was laid to rest in Detroit.

†

3

CHARTING THE COURSE

"Unless we know about something that occurred years back and how people have set the stage for what should be happening now, we won't know how to operationalize our dreams in the present. To operationalize dreams means to do something about what was started in the past. African-Americans should know that the momentum was started over 200 years ago and we shouldn't sit around and talk about what we can't do. We should now demonstrate what can be done. What can we do today?"

— Dr. Irene H. Brodie

Irene Hale attended the University of Arkansas at Blytheville and Lincoln University in Jefferson City, Missouri, where she studied developmental education. She was very athletic and outgoing. In college she competed in track and field as a sprinter, running the seventy-five yard dash. After moving to Robbins, Illinois, a Chicago suburb, she attended Chicago Teacher's College, currently Chicago State University, where she earned a bachelor's degree. Irene excelled at a fast pace, academically. Not only did her excellent, high level of academic performance allow her to advance grade levels ahead of many of her peers, but on April 19,1960, Irene was recognized and honored for her academic achievements as a member of Kappa Delta Pi, an education honors society. Irene represented a very small number of African-Americans who received such honorable recognition. She attended the University of Chicago and was awarded a Master of Science degree in Education in 1968. Irene would later go on to pursue a doctoral degree from Nova Southeastern University, based in Fort Lauderdale, Florida. Upon successful completion of Nova Southeastern University's doctoral program, Irene was awarded a doctorate degree in education. She added the professional designation to her name and was now acknowledged and referred to as "Dr. Irene Brodie."

For a short time, Irene served as a tutor and substitute teacher in Missouri, where she taught students in first through eighth grades in the Missouri Public School System. During the 1960s and 1970s, it was not uncommon for teachers to take physical disciplinary action in the classroom against unruly or disobedient students. However, Irene preferred not to discipline her students by physical punishment. Instead, she preferred to apply different, subtler techniques to charm her students and to persuade them to conduct themselves better. The methods she employed to help keep students obedient would later become the norm in school polices governing teacher conduct. Today, across the country, it is unlawful for any teacher or school faculty member to physically punish a child. In this regard, Irene was ahead of the times, and certainly ahead of some of her peers who taught in the classroom.

Irene Brodie taught sixth grade students at Thomas J. Kellar Middle School in Robbins, Illinois under the leadership of J.E. Brodie, who served as the school's principal, and whom would become her husband. Although Irene taught students at various grade levels, she spent a considerable amount of time teaching sixth grade students. She also taught students at the Delia M. Turner Elementary School in Robbins. It was there that she was promoted to the position of assistant principal.

While serving as the assistant principal of Turner Elementary School, Irene was recruited to teach English at Harold L. Richards High School, which was predominantly white and located in the community of Oak Lawn, Illinois. Irene served as a member of the Libra School Board for fourteen years, helping to provide for the education and the personal needs of special needs children. She served as president for three years and as secretary for four years. Irene also served four terms as president, and three terms as secretary of the Illinois Two-Year College Reading Teachers Association.

4

J. E. BRODIE

"The need of an education is a vital necessity in our present, changing social order...Remember these words: 'Not to the swift is the crown of life, but to he who endureth to the end.'"

— *J. E. Brodie*
Principal, Thomas J. Kellar Middle School

❧

While teaching in Missouri, Irene would meet Judge Edmon "J.E." Brodie. Born May 22, 1906, Judge would adopt his initials "J.E." as a nickname to prevent people from mistaking him for being a judge, an officer of the court. Soon after adopting his initials as his nickname, he was referred to as "J.E." The two first met at a social event where J.E. served as a chaperone to students at a high school affair. J.E. was immediately attracted to Irene and inquired about her age. Upon discovering that Irene was just seventeen years old at the time, he decided to wait before courting her. He told her, "I'm coming back for you."

Judge Edmon "J.E." Brodie was a principal at Hayti Negro High School, a local community high school in Hayti, Missouri that would ultimately become desegregated as a result of the landmark U.S. Supreme Court decision *Brown v. Board of Education*, which banned segregation in education. Hayti Negro High School was subsequently renamed "Hayti Central High School," following the decision handed down by the U.S. Supreme Court in the case of *Brown v. Board of Education*.

J.E. also taught college-level evening courses in education, where Irene was a student of his. J.E. immediately recognized Irene as being exceptionally talented, and as one of his most accomplished and gifted students. He was in awe of Irene's thirst for knowledge and her unrelenting dedication and determination to achieve and excel academically. His background in education allowed him to immediately recognize Irene's talent and dedication as a teacher. Attracted to each other from the moment they met, their love for one another grew even stronger within a few months. J.E. found Irene to be very beautiful, classy, as well as an exceptionally academically gifted young woman. Irene said she was attracted to J.E's charm and good looks. He was a very mature and wise gentleman, as he was just entering the middle-age period of his life. J.E was considerably older than Irene and, in fact, had a daughter nearly the same age as Irene. Having become a member of Kappa Alpha Psi Fraternity while in college, J.E. kept himself well groomed and was a meticulous dresser. He was also academically gifted, and had earned a Master of Science degree from Southern Illinois University in Carbondale, Illinois on August 5, 1949.

J.E. Brodie moved to Illinois to serve as Principal of Thomas J. Kellar Middle School in Robbins, Illinois, a small suburb just fifteen miles southwest of Chicago. After spending a short time in Illinois pursuing career opportunities in education, J.E. returned to Missouri to propose to Irene. The two became officially engaged, and soon thereafter married on July 31, 1954 in a ceremony at St. Louis City Hall administered by a Justice of the Peace. J.E.'s marriage to Irene was his second.

J.E.'s first wife passed away shortly after their divorce. J.E. fathered one child with his first wife, a daughter, who was named Arnetta. Irene and Arnetta were very close in age, with only a year or two separating them. As J.E. and Irene's romantic relationship began to flourish, Irene often found herself being the subject of ridicule and condescending remarks made by J.E.'s mother, Ada Murphy, who had on several occasions expressed to Irene that she was not fond of her son keeping company with a "skinny girl with such a dark complexion." J.E.'s mother was a very light-skinned black woman who ardently professed that her complexion was an indicator of not only class and privilege, but entitlement as well. Irene recalled the time when Mrs. Murphy offered her a white cream to apply to her face to "lighten" her skin complexion. "You look like you've been working outside in the hot sun all day, honey," Murphy said. Despite the sometimes uncomfortable and awkward encounters that she experienced with her soon-to-be mother-in-law, Irene, for the sake of her relationship with J.E., chose to turn the other cheek when comments about the "darkness" of her skin persisted. She was determined to win Mrs. Murphy's love and acceptance by acting "lady-like" and maintaining her politeness and respect.

Mr. Brodie was a pioneer in helping to integrate the teaching staff at schools where he taught and served as an administrator. As a college instructor and school administrator, he opened the door for African-Americans and other minorities to enter the profession of teaching, and assisted some with obtaining other employment opportunities in education. He was instrumental in giving many local African-American teachers, as well as others from across the nation, their start in teaching careers. Mr. Brodie recruited some candidates for teacher positions from Missouri, where he had established himself as a prominent educator, to fill open positions at schools in Illinois, where he served as principal. He was credited with recruiting some very talented educators who excelled in the profession and became very notable, including Mr. Otto M. Bradford who ultimately succeeded Mr. Brodie as principal of Thomas J. Kellar Middle School, and James Charles Evers, civil rights activist and older brother of slain civil rights leader Medgar Evers. When Charles Evers ran into trouble with the Ku Klux Klan in Mississippi, he fled the state and relocated to Illinois where J.E. hired him as a teacher at Kellar Middle School. Evers taught seventh grade students and was recognized for his in-depth knowledge and proficiency in teaching black history. In fact, it is said that Evers abruptly vacated his teacher position at Kellar Middle School on the day that his brother, Medgar was assassinated, in order to return to Mississippi. In the year 1969, James Charles Evers earned his place in history by becoming the first African-American since the Reconstruction Era to have been elected mayor of a city in Mississippi, the City of Fayette in Jefferson County.

Mr. J.E. Brodie was also an influential force in helping Irene gain various teaching positions within the local school district where he served as principal, and as history will attest, Irene became quite a trailblazer herself and arguably, J.E.'s most notable professional recruit.

J.E. Brodie served as Principal of Thomas J. Kellar Middle School from years 1954 through 1957 before being recruited by a Chicago area high school district to serve as principal. Not long after leaving his position at Kellar Middle School, J.E.'s mother, Ada Hickman Murphy, passed away.

J.E. Brodie was later recruited by High School District 218 to serve as Principal of Blue Island Community High School, which would later be renamed Dwight D. Eisenhower High School. Mr. Brodie served at the Southeast Campus Building. The Southeast Campus represented an all-black branch of Eisenhower High School, and offered classes to students in their first two years of high school. The "Old Main" building located in Blue Island, Illinois was where white students in their freshman and sophomore years attended classes at Eisenhower High. Upon advancing to the junior grade level, black students in Robbins were bussed to neighboring Blue Island where the main campus of Eisenhower High School was located. White students who advanced grade levels at Old Main, were also transferred to Eisenhower's main campus. This period in the late 1950s and early 1960s was a time when the environment at the main campus was often hostile towards black students, as racial tensions were rising with increased integration on the heels of the Supreme Court decision in *Brown v. Board of Education*. J.E. Brodie served as Principal at the Southeast Campus from 1957 through 1966. He was recognized, posthumously, on October 22, 2011, by the Class of 1961 for his leadership, guidance, and contribution to the education of Robbins' youth.

Dr. Irene Brodie was a trailblazer on the front line as a teacher during the tumultuous time in our nation's history when schools were undergoing racial integration. Irene was recruited to teach English at Richards High School, a predominantly white school in Oak Lawn, Illinois, a predominantly white suburb of Chicago. This was a first, primarily because students at this school were not accustomed to having a black teacher. Irene embraced the challenges that came with the nation's period of desegregation. Teaching students in the Oak Lawn community provided her with a springboard, which demonstrated not only her exceptional capabilities as a dedicated teacher, but also showed that her knowledge and poise could transcend the barriers of race that existed and caused division in classrooms across America.

After teaching English at Richards High School for about three years, Irene decided to accept an offer to teach college-level courses at a nearby, newly founded community college, Moraine Valley Community College. Moraine Valley was formed to fill a need in the sprawling South Suburban region for an additional institution of higher learning. It was here that she was able to springboard her teaching career to an advanced level for higher learning. Irene Brodie would also prove to be irreplaceable in leading the efforts by the newly formed college in developing and writing some of its initial curriculum and its formulation of diverse, rigorous educational programs.

Also during this time, J.E. and Irene Brodie commissioned a prominent black homebuilder, Edward Starks, to build their dream home in their new hometown of Robbins, Illinois. Starks, a Robbins native who attended the University of Illinois and studied engineering, had returned to his native home to build houses. He developed many of the more affluent homes in the village, in an area later known as Golden Acres. Since Starks built most of the homes in this area, many residents still refer to them as the "Starks Homes."

Shortly after moving to Illinois in 1954, Irene and J.E. joined Great Hope Missionary Baptist Church in Robbins. Despite having an unwavering dedication to her faith, Irene would have it tested in ways that she could never have imagined. In 1966, she lost J.E. to a heart attack.

During this most difficult period of time in her life, Irene relied on her faith to sustain her.

†

5

HISTORIC ROBBINS, ILLINOIS

"...It started with families of interracial marriages of people who lived in Chicago and were not treated well by either racial group. They chose to look for an escape so they could live their lives in peace and tranquility, and people moved out here. As the years went on, predominantly African-Americans moved out here."

—Dr. Irene H. Brodie

Robbins, Illinois is a small, quiet town, located approximately fifteen miles southwest of Chicago. Incorporated on December 14, 1917, it is the oldest all-black governed and incorporated town in the northern half of the United States. It is distinctly recognized as one of only a very small group of towns founded, organized, and governed by blacks in the entire country. The town was founded by three black men: Thomas J. Kellar, who led the effort, accompanied by Richard Flowers, and LeRoy P. Thomas. The residents of this unincorporated area of Cook County, Illinois sought to protect themselves and their property from citizens of surrounding towns, and to provide themselves with the necessary services required for a growing settlement. Having worked at the Cook County Assessor's Office in downtown Chicago, Thomas J. Kellar was assigned the task of investigating the procedures for incorporation. Thomas J. Kellar served as the town's first mayor, and co-founder, Richard Flowers was subsequently elected to serve as the town's third mayor.

Robbins, located within Bremen and Worth Townships, is situated on approximately one and one-half square miles of land. Prior to being settled on, it was largely farmland owned and controlled by white real estate investors, and land speculators who had acquired the land in anticipation of the City of Chicago, located just minutes away, expanding its boundaries by annexing the land to accommodate the World's Columbian Exposition in 1893.

The hopes of the investors and land speculators were dashed when the World's Columbian Exposition came and left Chicago, without the city annexing the land and expanding its borders that far south. What some land investors and speculators had built up in anticipation of a boom, had now turned into a bust. The high land prices once paid by speculators proved in some instances to be a total loss. Many owners, as they attempted to sell, were unable to get anywhere near the prices they had initially paid. Some of them held on to their land until the property taxes were nearly equal to the price initially paid, and either sold at a loss or forfeited their land entirely to the government for back taxes.

Despite the misfortune experienced by many white investors, resulting from the non-acquisition of the vacant land by the City of Chicago, one white real estate investor, Henry E. Robbins, and two of his sons, Frank G. Robbins and Eugene S. Robbins, saw opportunity and decided to acquire it. Henry had the desire to help people of color become owners of land and property. He enticed several persons of color to settle on some of the abandoned lots, which he sold to them for as little as ninety dollars on a monthly installment payment plan. The lots were sold at such a cheap price because they did not have plumbing or sewer lines.

Inadequate plumbing did not pose a problem for most blacks, whom, in many cases, had migrated from the South and were accustomed to living in homes that lacked state-of the-art plumbing and sewer lines. Although colored settlers moved into the area as early as 1892, growth of the settlement slowed down tremendously until Henry E. Robbins established his first subdivision. Robbins' efforts proved to be such a success that he opened up his first subdivision in 1910. Soon thereafter, he sold all of the lots within that subdivision. As a result of their father's success, sons Frank and Eugene followed suit by building several subdivisions of their own. So explosive was the growth in population during the years between 1911 and 1917, more than 300 people were now living within the adjoining subdivisions. Eugene S. Robbins, who took over after his father died, built eight subdivisions, while his brother, Frank, built one subdivision.

As the population continued to grow, the concern for maintaining law and order soon became an issue of great concern. The question of incorporating was raised. One of the early settlers, Samuel E. Nichols, organized a club of sorts that addressed not only political concerns, but civic and other concerns of interest to the overall community. This organization evolved into what was known as the "Robbins Political and Social Club." The organization elected Richard Flowers to serve as its president. Mr. Flowers consulted with and sought the assistance of a community activist, Thomas J. Kellar, who also worked at the County Assessor's Office to investigate the necessary steps and requirements of incorporating a village. Upon receiving the necessary information and meeting the necessary criteria, the club voted to officially organize as a village.

Not everyone supported the village incorporating; some even campaigned against it. A petition was drawn up and presented to the county court, asking for an election to determine the proposition. The presiding judge set Tuesday, December 11, 1917, as the day of the election. Although organized opposition fought hard against incorporating the village, the measure in favor of incorporating passed by a wide margin. On December 14, 1917, by order of the court, Robbins was officially declared a village, thus making it a municipal corporation and an independent body of local government.

The Village of Robbins, now an official municipal corporation, was duly chartered by the State of Illinois, and organized under the State of Illinois for the purpose of providing its residents with a number of services, including police protection, fire protection, water service, sanitary and storm sewer service, maintenance of streets and sidewalks, community and economic development, public transportation, building inspections, and municipal code enforcement.

Robbins quickly became a growing and prosperous village where black and mixed-race individuals and families were able to live and pursue the American Dream. During the early 1900s, legalized social inequalities were not only the norm in the South, but it was all too common in the northern part of the United States as well, especially in Illinois—the "Land of Lincoln." The newly founded Village of Robbins offered unlimited hope without boundaries to the many blacks, mulattoes, and interracial couples that dared to move there and stake their claim as property and business owners.

The Village of Robbins was cast into the international spotlight when Marcus Garvey, the Jamaican-born, world renowned political activist, selected Robbins as the site where he would hold his Chicago-area rallies. In the 1920s, Garvey used Calvary Hall, located at 3349 West 139th Street, to launch his Back-To-Africa Movement. Garvey believed that racism was a permanent fixture in American society and that African-Americans would never truly attain equal rights in the United States.

Having founded the Universal Negro Improvement Association (UNIA), Garvey saw Robbins as a model town, representing what blacks in America could accomplish by liberating themselves politically and economically, while making Africa inclusive in the movement.

Robbins served as such an impetus for hope and opportunity for African-Americans that by the early 1930s, the village was boasting itself as being the home of the first airport in the nation that was owned, constructed, and operated by blacks. This bold initiative by blacks in aviation clearly paved the way for other blacks who were denied the opportunity to fly and pursue careers in aviation elsewhere, to now don their wings. The Robbins Airport allowed black pilots to land and take off at a time when they were being denied flying and landing rights at most white owned and operated airports in the country, including those in nearby Chicago. Racism directed at black pilots often caused some of them to fly into the Robbins Airport and be arrested by white police officers from some of the neighboring towns surrounding Robbins. These communities decried black pilots flying in the airspace over their towns, and would routinely dispatch their police officers to arrest the black pilots once they landed at the Robbins Airport.

Robbins is certainly a national treasure being home to the first black owned and operated airport in the nation. The airport also served as a major training facility for black pilots. At that time, Robbins was home to one of the only flight schools in the nation where African-Americans were trained as pilots, and home to a flight school that served as a model for the Tuskegee Airmen Program during World War Two (WWII).

In fact, nearly a dozen of the original Tuskegee Airmen were residents of Robbins. The late Cornelius R. Coffey and John C. Robinson built the Robbins Airport. They were both inspired by Chicagoan Bessie Coleman, a black female aviation pioneer. Both men were also among the first blacks to shatter the ceiling of discrimination by enrolling and graduating from the Curtiss-Wright Aeronautical University in Chicago, earning certificates in flight and aircraft mechanics. In 1931, Masseurs Coffey and Robinson put their knowledge to work by constructing the nation's first black owned and operated airport and flight training school, in Robbins, Illinois. This airport served as the aviation center in the North for African-Americans in aviation. The single runway and hangar airport was located at 14046 South Lawndale Avenue.

The Robbins Airport and flight training school's first airplane was purchased with the help of Janet Harmon-Bragg, one of the nation's first black female pilots. The Robbins Airport and training school had been operational for three years when, in 1933, the single hangar airport and all three airplanes inside were destroyed by a tornado. This natural disaster caused all aviation training to be provided at an alternative airport right outside of Chicago. The flight school and its operations were relocated by the invitation of white owners of the 87th and Harlem Airport in unincorporated Worth Township, just southwest of present-day Midway International Airport in Chicago. From there, many of the flight school instructors entered the Tuskegee Airmen Program. One notable instructor was John C. Robinson, who entered WWII as Supreme Commander of the Royal Ethiopian Air Force. The activities of these men and women have been recognized by the Smithsonian Institution's Air and Space Museum.

At present, a commemorative marker stands on the site where the Robbins Airport once stood in recognition of the achievements and contributions of the pioneering black aviators. Ten of the original Tuskegee Airmen called Robbins their home – Major General Lucius Theus, Marshall Knox, Clarence Dougan, Elbert "Zip" Johnson, Flarzell Moore, Sr., William Nowlin, Lawrence Shelby, Homer Ward, Edward Willett, Jr., and Dan Williamson. More recently, another resident of Robbins had a significant impact on the United States' Space Exploration Program. The National Aeronautics Space Administration (NASA) enlisted the help of Nichelle Nichols, a nationally renowned African-American actress, to assist NASA with attracting and recruiting qualified African-American candidates to join its Space Exploration Program. This program, instituted by NASA, would ultimately lead to the successful recruitment of Dr. Mae Jemison, Ronald McNair, and other highly esteemed African-American astronauts that have contributed greatly to the success of our nation's Space Exploration Program.

Grace Nichelle Nichols was appointed to the Board of Directors of the National Space Institute. Nichelle Nichols is the daughter of the late Samuel Earl Nichols, who was a chemist, inventor, and also served as the fourth mayor of Robbins, Illinois from 1929 to 1931. She also starred in the hit television series *Star Trek* as Lieutenant Uhura. According to an article published by The Wall Street Journal, Dr. Martin Luther King was a huge fan of *Star Trek's* Lieutenant Uhura, and it was his words of encouragement, and his explaining the value of Nichelle's Trek role to the African-American people during the Civil Rights Era to her, that influenced her decision to not leave the television series at the end of its first season.

Robbins, Illinois was the home of S.B. Fuller, president and founder of the Fuller Products Company. Mr. Fuller rose from poverty to millionaire status by selling soap and cosmetic products door-to-door. During the 1950s, Mr. Fuller was believed to be the richest African-American man in the United States. His cosmetics company had a reported $10 million in sales annually, and boasted a sales force positioned throughout 38 states and numbering around five thousand personnel, one-third of which were white. Mr. Fuller not only sold the products himself, he also built the business and accomplished all this with just a sixth grade education. S.B. Fuller was a pioneer in black economic development, and a trailblazer in sales and network marketing. He entrusted and provided independent salespeople with products to make their initial sales. He believed that once successful, the sales force would return for more products and pay him for products that were advanced. Fuller's sales and networking strategy were very successful and earned him national acclaim. With the headquarters of his business located in the near South Side of Chicago in the 2700 block of South Wabash Avenue, Mr. Fuller gave inspiration and training to countless aspiring entrepreneurs, including the likes of the late John H. Johnson, the founder of Ebony and Jet magazines, and George Johnson, the founder of Johnson Products Company, the beauty and cosmetics conglomerate. Mr. Fuller had his home, the S.B. Fuller Mansion, built in Robbins in 1958 at 135th Street and Kedzie Avenue. Fuller's prairie-style house, which still stands today, was built for the then unheard of sum of $250,000.

Mr. Fuller was also a successful publisher. *The New York Age* and *Pittsburgh Courier* were two of his most recognized publications. S.B. Fuller was a self-proclaimed Republican, an example and staunch advocate of self-help, or as the saying goes, "pulling one's self up by his own bootstraps." Mr. Fuller had a very significant impact on the Village of Robbins, where he played a major part in helping to facilitate the construction of the village's first water tower and water distribution station. He loaned a few of his lawyers, and money to the village, which ultimately enabled the Village of Robbins to tie in to the City of Chicago's water distribution line. This accomplishment positioned Robbins at the forefront of the South Suburbs with a reliable and high quality water system, and not all suburban communities, particularly in the South Suburbs, could boast of having such a high quality water system.

From the beginning, Robbins has welcomed blacks and mixed-race people who fled the South Side of Chicago and other areas of the region in order to escape racial bigotry. Robbins, as one of the oldest all-black governed towns in the United States and only one of two such towns in the State of Illinois, and the only one in the Chicago metropolitan area, had been for a very long time the only south suburb where blacks were openly welcomed to live, as well as own and operate businesses.

†

6

JERAYE

"Mom, when I finish my bachelor's degree, I'm going to come back and work with Robbins. Somebody's got to get out there and do it."

—*Jeraye Evelyn Brodie*

Few things can bring more joy to the eyes of a parent than the birth of a child. On April 17, 1957, J.E. and Irene became the proud parents of a baby girl, Jeraye Evelyn Brodie. Irene gave birth to Jeraye at 6:39 p.m. at the University of Chicago Hospital. In anticipation of the child's birth, J.E. and Irene had chosen the name, "Jerald" in the event the baby was born a boy and "Jeraye" in the event the baby was born a girl. J.E. requested to name their newborn daughter so that her initials would reflect his, and Irene agreed. Jeraye Evelyn Brodie was the name given to the newborn baby girl by her father. Jeraye would be the only child that J.E. and Irene would have together.

Balancing the responsibilities of a new mother, wife, homemaker, and career woman offered many challenges for Irene. J.E.'s responsibilities as a principal at Thomas J. Kellar Middle School consumed much of his time as well. Both J.E. and Irene realized that they would have to make some necessary sacrifices so that they could provide the very best childcare for Jeraye, while allowing them to continue pursuing their careers. Irene's youngest sister, Bertha Lee Hale, would often serve as Jeraye's caretaker when J.E. and Irene needed the extra help. This arrangement proved to be the ideal solution to their childcare needs, because Mr.

and Mrs. Brodie attained the capable and trusted help of Bertha, not to mention the fact that she and Jeraye got along perfectly well together. This allowed for J.E. and Irene to be the good and loving parents they were determined to be, at the same time, being able to focus on their careers, which seemed to require an unlimited amount of time. This arrangement worked out well for Auntie Bertha too because babysitting helped her earn extra money for college.

As a little girl, Jeraye made an appearance on the very popular *Bozo Circus* show with Bozo the Clown, which aired on Channel 9, WGN-TV in Chicago.

Known affectionately as "Stuffy" by her parents and close friends, Jeraye would demonstrate early on that she would follow in her parents' footsteps by excelling academically. Her dedication and passion for her schoolwork not only earned her honors, but also placed her on the fast track for college preparation. Jeraye attended Dwight D. Eisenhower High School in Blue Island, Illinois, a community adjacent to Robbins. Jeraye excelled in her academic studies at Eisenhower and was a member of the Eisenhower Cardinals marching band. She played the French horn and was also a gifted pianist. Like her mother, Jeraye entered college at age sixteen and advanced to become a senior by the time she reached age nineteen. She was multi-lingual, having become fluent in French and Spanish.

After a challenging day of school and extra-curricular activities, Jeraye always seemed to find a little more time in the day to enjoy her passion for playing the organ. She also gave a lot of time and attention to her pet dog, "Pepsi." Pepsi was a Chihuahua with a shiny black coat of hair, hence the name, Pepsi. Jeraye was three years old when her dad decided to surprise her with the puppy, and together, they decided on the dog's name. Of course, the puppy's shiny black coat influenced her name, but J.E's love of the soft drink was at least an equally contributing factor. Jeraye was just excited that her dad had given her a puppy. From that day on, it seemed she and Pepsi were inseparable.

Jeraye shared her parents' love for education and helping those who were less fortunate toward breaking through economic and social barriers. She joined her parents in their mission to better educate, and make higher learning available to, Robbins area students by offering tutoring after school. Jeraye excelled academically and wanted to help empower other youngsters who faced challenges in their studies.

Jeraye enjoyed producing puppet shows for the children at the Delia Turner Elementary School where her mom served as a teacher and assistant principal in the early 1960s. She enjoyed working with grade school students, and because she possessed such a natural talent for working with children, many expected her to follow in her parents' footsteps and pursue a career in education.

In 1967, Irene and Jeraye met family members as they arrived by train in Chicago from Kansas City to embark on a memorable journey to the 1967 Montreal Expo. The family traveled by train from Chicago to Detroit, where they were met by Ethel and her husband, Zell. From there, much of the entire family continued their journey by train to Montreal, Canada.

Jeraye occasionally enjoyed driving her car on short road trips. She drove two of her friends, Elbert Mock and Leticia Davis, to St. Louis for a weekend getaway at Six Flags over Mid-America. She often drove to Kansas City with her mother during summer breaks and Christmas holidays to visit family members. Both Elbert and Leticia were good friends of Jeraye. Leticia was one of her closest girlfriends, and Elbert and Jeraye were high school sweethearts. Elbert had been a student of Irene's when she taught at Turner Elementary School, and Irene was fond of Elbert, as he was one her most exceptional students. Elbert and Jeraye courted throughout high school, attending their high school sock hop and prom together.

After attending several outings and brief vacations, Jeraye observed that she began to consistently experience symptoms of fatigue even though she had not over-exerted herself physically. She also suffered from fevers that were unexplainable. She was taken to the hospital for a medical evaluation, and it was determined that she suffered from Lupus.

Systemic Lupus Erythematosus (SLE) is a collection of autoimmune diseases, in which the human immune system becomes hyperactive and attacks normal, healthy tissues, causing inflammation, swelling, pain, and organ damage.

According to medical authorities, nine out of ten people that develop Lupus are women. Jeraye's battle with Lupus was a long and painful one. Her battle brought about very noticeable changes in her physical appearance, including chronic loss of energy, loss of hair, and significant weight gain.

Despite all of the pain, the trials, and tribulations, Jeraye stayed focused on her academics. She always kept a very positive attitude and her determination to succeed was never higher. She never let go of her dreams and she never stopped pursuing them. Jeraye even occasionally visited area children's hospitals to befriend young children who were afflicted with life-threatening illnesses.

Jeraye was a very smart and observant young child. She recognized early on that some of the things that came easy for her presented much more of a challenge for many of her peers. Jeraye realized that she was fortunate to have a good upbringing in a family where she was an only child with both loving parents who were both accomplished and distinguished educators, and who could afford to provide her with the very best things in life. Since both parents were successful educators, nothing less than academic excellence was expected of Jeraye.

Growing up in a community like Robbins, Jeraye often witnessed several of her friends struggle. Some of them struggled academically and lacked certain resources to improve their performance. Some of them lacked the financial resources to afford proper clothing, shoes, and books, attend school field trips, and in too many cases, even lacked money to pay for their breakfast or lunch. Many of the things that Jeraye had immediate access to with no worry, she witnessed some of her friends struggle for on a daily basis. Jeraye wanted so badly for all of her friends and peers to enjoy the same socio-economic benefits she had become accustomed to enjoying in her life. Jeraye drew the attention of both her parents when she began to frequently request to volunteer to tutor some of her classmates, and when she would request to participate in school sponsored events, such as bake sales and other fundraisers aimed at generating money to help students who were in dire need of one thing or another.

Jeraye's relentless efforts to help many of her fellow classmates and neighborhood friends had a profound and lasting impact on both her parents, especially Irene. J.E. became even more determined to help high school students where he served as principal to obtain scholarships so they could pursue a college education. Working closely with Jeraye, Irene became even more involved in community service activities. Jeraye's aspirations and efforts to help those in her community was so powerful that Irene credits her daughter with being the catalyst that inspired her to commit a large part of her life to public service. When Jeraye became a teenager, she would occasionally say to Irene, "Mom, when I finish my bachelor's degree, I'm going to come back and work with Robbins. Somebody's got to get out there and do it."

Jeraye not only enjoyed academic success but she was also well liked by her peers and friends. She enjoyed a social life that included a very loving group. She attended Lincoln Memorial School in Robbins, Eisenhower High School, and Illinois Wesleyan University in Bloomington, Illinois for her first two years of college. In 1975, she transferred to Barat College in Lake Forest, Illinois to complete her studies. It was in her senior year while attending Barat College that Jeraye's long, and oftentimes painful, battle with Lupus claimed her life. Jeraye's battle ended at LaRabida Hospital in Chicago at approximately 7:00 a.m. on Friday, September 10, 1976. Jeraye Evelyn Brodie was only nineteen years old.

The day Irene lost her only child would be the most difficult day of her life. A new resident who had just moved to the neighborhood within a few doors of the Brodie residence was startled the morning she heard a loud scream from a woman standing in the back yard of her home. The neighbor walked over to offer assistance and learned that the woman in distress was Irene. "My baby died! My baby died," Irene continued to scream as a steady stream of tears ran down her face. This day would spiral Irene into a deep depression from which it would take her years to recover. In the years following Jeraye's passing, Irene left Jeraye's belongings untouched, including the outfit that she had laid out for Jeraye to wear during an upcoming visit. Irene confided in a few close friends and colleagues that in losing both J.E. and Jeraye, she had lost her will to live. In fact, during an interview with Sunya Walls, a reporter for the *South Suburban Citizen* newspaper, Irene stated,

"I have no family in Robbins. I'm an only person there. My husband died of a heart attack in 1966. We had one child and she died in 1976, when she was a senior in college. She died from a disease called Lupus. I lost her and that was the end of my family. I had a wipeout in Robbins. My thought was, I didn't have a reason to get up in the morning. I didn't have a reason to live. I said lots of prayers and asked God to give me a reason for being."

†

7

MORAINE VALLEY

"Educating the children of Robbins is an important priority of the village. We educate our children very strongly in Robbins. They have become lawyers, doctors, accountants, and executives of insurance companies."

—*Dr. Irene H. Brodie*

Moraine Valley Community College (MVCC), located just twenty-five minutes southwest of Chicago in suburban Palos Hills, Illinois, was established in 1967. In 1965, members of the Oak Lawn Rotary Club initiated efforts to establish the community college. In 1966, a steering committee was formed to study the proposed junior college district, projected enrollment, and financial possibilities. A petition to form a community college district was submitted to the Illinois Junior College Board in Springfield, Illinois. Soon thereafter, the Illinois Junior College Board and the Illinois Board of Education approved the establishment of a community college district for the Southwest Suburbs.

In 1967, area residents passed a referendum approving the formation of a community college, and an election created Community College District 524 and its first seven trustees. Theodore F. Lownik was named Board Chairman. The college was officially created after two years of proposals, approvals, and planning, officially opening its first temporary office in Oak Lawn, Illinois. Initially, classes were held in leased warehouses in Alsip, Illinois. The main campus of the college is now located in the valley nestled in the Cook County Forest Preserves, sprawling over 294 acres. The college also operates satellite facilities in Blue Island and Tinley Park, both suburbs located in the Chicago Southland area. Moraine Valley has a present-day enrollment of over 35,000 students, making it the second largest community college in the State of Illinois.

Irene H. Brodie established herself as a talented and respected teacher by both her students and her peers in the teaching profession. This leadership was recognized by the founders of the newly developed Moraine Valley Community College. Irene was teaching nearby at Harold L. Richards High School in Oak Lawn, near the temporary offices where Moraine Valley Community College was located, when she was sought out by the founders of Moraine Valley to not only serve as an instructor, but also to assist with developing the curriculum for the college. Dr. Brodie founded the Academic Skills Center at Moraine Valley. Dr. Brodie served as assistant professor of communications for two years, from 1968 to 1970. She was promoted to the administrative post of director of the Academic Skills Center. Dr. Brodie managed grants for the college and monitored the success of students. Attaining a high student retention rate was one of Dr. Brodie's main objectives, and she is credited with having achieved great success in this area. Dr. Brodie was relentless in her efforts to help students achieve and succeed in their academic programs. Her concern for and dedication to the students were unparalleled.

Dr. Brodie was known for fighting for the rights of students who were academically challenged. College staff and students all agreed that Dr. Brodie truly cared about the success of students, as was demonstrated by her successfully serving in this position for eleven years. Her demonstrated leadership would soon earn her the distinguished position and title of Dean of Educational Development.

During some of the most challenging times of her life, Dr. Brodie gives credit, in large part, to many of her colleagues at Moraine Valley Community College, especially the college president, Dr. Vernon Crawley, for oftentimes encouraging and motivating her to achieve her absolute greatest achievements. 'You can do it. I know you can do it, Dr. Brodie,' she often quoted her colleagues as saying. As Dean of Developmental Education, Dr. Brodie played a critical role in managing grants awarded to the college.

Dr. Brodie played an instrumental role at Moraine Valley by establishing satellite facilities in Robbins and Blue Island, Illinois. Moraine Valley leased space in the Community and Economic Development Association (CEDA) building, where the college offered courses in lobotomy, computer programming, and general educational development (GED) basic skills. The Robbins facility offered ideal access to college-bound residents of the village. Moraine Valley's Robbins satellite facility was so successful that the college outgrew its space in the CEDA building and had to relocate to nearby Blue Island to accommodate its increased student enrollment.

Dr. Brodie helped Moraine Valley with diversification of the college's staff. Located in Palos Hills and surrounded by similar all-white communities during the early years of the college's existence, Moraine Valley initially faced challenges with recruiting African-Americans and other minorities to serve on its staff. The predominantly white communities that surrounded the Moraine Valley college campus were not very welcoming to African-American students or staff that traveled through the communities on their way to the college campus. This concern often deterred qualified minority applicants from pursuing and accepting employment opportunities with the college, as finding quality housing for minorities within close proximity to the Moraine Valley campus was difficult at times.

While serving as Dean of Educational Development at Moraine Valley, Dr. Brodie was able to oversee a joint project between Moraine Valley and the Posen-Robbins School District 143 ½. The Posen-Robbins School District was where Dr. Brodie first taught early in her career. Dr. Brodie was elated to participate in a joint project between the school district and Moraine Valley. Moraine Valley received a $45,000 award from former First Lady Barbara Bush, on behalf of her Foundation for Family Literacy. This project was aimed at motivating first and second graders and their families to read together for fun. Approximately twenty-five parents and fifty children initially participated in the project and provided an environment that enabled parents to get directly involved in their child's learning process. The project enabled instructors, provided by Moraine Valley, to start out working with students and parents separately, and then bring them together. Parenting, reading, and discipline were topics of group discussion among the families. Through the discussions, lessons were written and processed. The focus was aimed at promoting ongoing discussions so that solutions could be found for academic and social concerns. The grant from the Barbara Bush Foundation allowed Moraine Valley to expand this program from a half-year to a full year project.

Dr. Brodie was a staunch advocate of working with young children and their parents. Children in the Posen-Robbins School District were referred to the program based on their academic and behavioral needs.

In the year 2000, the Moraine Valley Automotive Technology Department was designated as an official Daimler-Chrysler CAP (Chrysler Apprenticeship Program) training center for the Chicagoland area. Dr. Brodie recognized and seized this opportunity to recruit students from Robbins who were aspiring to become automobile mechanics. While serving Moraine Valley as Dean of Educational Development, Dr. Brodie, who had become Mayor of Robbins by this time, was able to identify various educational and economic opportunities that many of the residents of the Village of Robbins would be able to benefit from.

Dr. Brodie had established a successful track record of providing a bridge of opportunity to the community, expanding from Moraine Valley to Robbins, Illinois. Moraine Valley provided new computers to Robbins' William Leonard Public Library as part of a continuing partnership between Moraine Valley Community College and the Village of Robbins.

After having served as an assistant professor, administrator, and Dean of Educational Development at Moraine Valley for thirty-two years, Dr. Brodie retired from her position at the college in the year 2000. At the beginning of the new millennium, Dr. Brodie decided to focus more of her attention on the needs of the youth in the Village of Robbins, where she had at that point successfully served thirteen years as the mayor of the village. During her tenure at Moraine Valley, Dr. Brodie played a significant role in assisting the college with diversifying not only its student body, but its staff as well. The Moraine Valley Board of Trustees hired Dr. Vernon Crawley to serve as college president, the first African-American to ever serve in that position. Dr. Crawley's recruitment by Moraine Valley opened the door wide open for successfully recruiting African-Americans and other minorities to serve on the college's staff. Upon the retirement of Dr. Crawley, Dr. Jenkins, an African-American woman, was hired to succeed Dr. Crawley as president of Moraine Valley. In addition, the college's executive leadership team had grown to comprise nearly fifty percent minorities. Based on its success with diversification of its staff, Moraine Valley was awarded the "Higher Education Excellence and Diversity Award" by *INSIGHT into Diversity* magazine.

Shortly after Dr. Irene Brodie retired from her position as Dean of Moraine Valley Community College in the year 2001, the college named a wing in her honor. The Dr. Irene H. Brodie Academic Skills Center helps students improve their academic skills through an innovative support system. Mayor Brodie returned to Moraine Valley and became a benefactor to the college, donating $100,000. This generous gift is one of the largest ever contributed to the college by a member of its faculty. Dr. Brodie currently serves in the capacity of an adviser to, and a board member of, the Moraine Valley Community College Foundation.

†

8

HIDDEN IN PLAIN SIGHT

"Real integrity is doing the right thing, knowing that nobody is going to know whether you did it or not."

—*Oprah Winfrey*
Internationally Acclaimed
Television Talk Show Host
and Entrepreneur

During the time Dr. Brodie was teaching at Moraine Valley Community College and beginning her career in municipal government, serving as Clerk of the Village of Robbins, lawlessness in this community was spiraling out of control under the leadership of Mayor Marion L. Smith.

Mayor Marion Smith served three consecutive terms as mayor of Robbins, twelve years, from 1969 to 1981. During this time, Robbins saw an unprecedented level of corruption and criminal activity. The village had become a haven for chop shops. On average, the Robbins Police Department was recovering approximately twenty-five stripped and stolen automobile vehicles per month. The village had become a hub, if not *the* hub, of the South Suburbs for stolen vehicles and the selling of stolen auto body parts at illegal chop shops. Law enforcement officials identified several of these illegal shops operating in the village. These auto body shops used a significant number of juveniles to carry out their illegal activities. Presumably, the masterminds behind the illegal shops saw the use of minors as a way to evade the full potential of the penalties of the law once apprehended and prosecuted.

Prior to Dr. Brodie being elected mayor, widespread operations of chop shops, along with prostitution and gambling houses in Robbins, over time, made it clear that these illegal outfits must have had inside connections within the state power structure of the village. As soon as one outfit was disrupted by law enforcement, another would sprout up to take its place. Illegal gambling houses offered gamblers the ability to wage high-stakes bets on dice games, poker, and numbers which was an illegal lottery, as well as other outlawed activities. Oftentimes, the gambling houses also served as houses of prostitution. The illegal shops, in many cases, appeared to be operating as legitimate businesses because they were often fronted, and in some cases, operated by legitimate auto repair shops. Consequently, it was not alarming or unusual to witness the high volume of automobile traffic going in and out of those establishments. Suspicions grew that the chop shops must have had an inside track into the police department. Corruption became so prevalent that the Village Board of Trustees appointed a special investigator to look into possible wrongdoing within the ranks of the police department. The findings of the special investigator were indeed alarming; not only were members of the police department acting inappropriately, but the findings also clearly implicated the mayor himself.

It was alleged that Mayor Marion Smith was accepting kickbacks from chop shop operators, as much as $1,000 a month from one individual shop operator. According to insiders close to the special investigator, Mayor Smith would turn a blind eye to certain illegal operations that were paying him money, and he would instruct certain high-ranking members of the village's police department to do the same.

This conduct would provide cover for the illegal chop shops, gambling houses, and other illegal outfits to persist without interruption by local law enforcement. Routinely, those perpetrating criminal activity, were being tipped off by inside informants which kept them a few steps ahead of law enforcement.

When Mayor Smith was confronted with the findings of the specially appointed investigator, he accused the investigator of illegally impersonating a police officer. He challenged the validity of the Board of Trustees' action to appoint such a special investigator without his approval, and of the signing of a village ordinance approving the authorization of the appointment of the special investigator. The Board of Trustees refused to revoke its authorization of the special investigator appointment, so Mayor Smith refused to acknowledge the legitimacy of the special investigator empowered by the Village Board of Trustees. In an effort to curtail and thwart the efforts of the special investigator and any other members of the Robbins Police Department, Mayor Smith initiated efforts to do away with the entire police department. Insiders asserted that Mayor Smith was advised to take this action by one of the village attorneys. Mayor Smith and his attorney, Douglas Polsky, who advised the mayor to disband the police department, alleged that the mayor's primary reason for seeking to abolish the police department was due to widespread corruption within the department. Mayor Smith claimed that his intent was to abolish the department so that he could completely cleanse it of internal corruption.

Mayor Smith was often referred to as "The Big Man." He stood at approximately six feet and two inches tall, and weighed in at a little over three hundred pounds, earning him his nickname. Upon Robbins police officers investigating an illegal automobile chop shop, an operator and confidential informant told police that he was paying "The Big Man" $1,000 per month to operate in Robbins. Police investigators concluded from their investigations that the true identity of "The Big Man" was indeed Mayor Marion Smith. As police investigators strengthened their case, and as evidence that implicated wrongdoing by Mayor Smith mounted, actions taken by the mayor to abolish the police department became more expedient. Police officers who continued to build their case found themselves being the target of unwarranted disciplinary action by the top command of the police department. Disciplinary actions included suspension and outright termination of employment. These police officers were labeled as troublemakers and were accused of acting outside of departmental rules.

Mayor Smith governed with a heavy hand and was well able to earn his political capital, which enabled him to maintain a strong position as mayor by winning a third term. At the time, this election made him one of the longest serving mayors in the history of the Village of Robbins, and thereby enabled him to amass a tremendous amount of political capital and clout. During the normal course of business, if Mayor Smith wanted it done, it was done. He had very little tolerance for those who refused to play by the rules outlined in his political playbook. For those who resisted and refused to play along, he made sure they felt some form of repercussion for their disobedience.

On the evening of March 1, 1978, during a regularly scheduled city council meeting, Trustee John Hamilton, a staunch ally of Mayor Smith, motioned the council to adopt an ordinance to abolish the Robbins Police Department. Trustee William Ray seconded the motion. Trustee Richard Ballentine moved to table this motion until March 6, 1978. Trustee Mitchell Thomas seconded the motion. The motion to table the matter was voted on and received a split vote: three ayes and three nays—three for and three against. Acting in his capacity as Village President, to vote and serve as a tiebreaker, Mayor Smith stated that this matter was an emergency and voted NOT to table the motion.

The council meeting began to drag on late into the night. At 11:00 pm, after two trustees left the council chambers, the motion was voted on. Roll call for the vote on Ordinance number 3-1-78 was as follows: ayes: three; Trustees John Hamilton, William Ray, and Louis Rayon; nays: one; Trustee Richard Ballentine; absent: two; Trustees James Barnes and Mitchell Thomas. Ordinance number 3-1-78 had now been passed into law. The Robbins Police Department had officially been abolished. Never before in the recorded history of the United States, had a municipality voted to abolish its own police department. Public safety is one of the most vital services that a government provides to its citizens. This action by Mayor Smith and his allies in the city council drew the attention of media outlets across the nation. Many residents of the village were outraged as they and their property would be left without police protection. Ultimately, the Cook County Sheriff's Department was called in to provide public safety services, in the absence of Robbins police officers.

During Mayor Smith's Administration, problems at the water department went from bad to worse. One of Mayor Smith's predecessors, Mayor Theodore Hendricks, and the Village Board of Trustees made a Reconstruction Finance Loan (Series B Bond) in 1953 for the amount of $596,000. Between 1969 and 1972, Mayor Smith renegotiated the bond while serving his first term as mayor. The old Reconstruction Finance Bond for $596,000 was renegotiated, plus an additional $509,000 was secured, raising the bond total with unpaid interest and fees to $1.445 million. Interest payments after renegotiation were $28,900 and were payable every six months. The bonds issued were Water and Sewer Bonds, which were considered Revenue Bonds, and as such, it was required that the principle and interest owed on them be paid from revenue generated specifically by the water department.

Over a nine-year span, from 1969 to 1978, the following amounts were the only payments made on the bonds: $79,250 was paid out of the Village General Fund Account and $9,660 was paid from the Village General Fund Golden Prime Account. Neither of these were direct accounts of the water department. Only $32,907 was paid from the appropriate Water Fund Account. The total amount paid was equal to $121,817. The total amount that should have been paid was $520,200. The Village of Robbins was clearly woefully delinquent and in default with bond payments. The Ministers Conference of South Cook County, a citizen's action group, called for an outside investigation into the operations of the water department. That investigation yielded that bond payments were being disbursed from inappropriate village accounts. That discovery forced an end to village administrators being able to make future bond payments from accounts with money that was not derived from water department collections.

In 1981, the City of Chicago Water Department instituted a fifty-three percent rate hike for the Village of Robbins, along with dozens of other suburbs. Although the Village of Robbins and approximately fifty-three other municipalities joined in a class-action suit against the City of Chicago and its water department to prevent a rate hike, ultimately the City of Chicago prevailed in the matter, to the detriment of the Village of Robbins, causing it to become even more delinquent with its water bill payments to the City of Chicago and other vendors.

Mayor Marion Smith attempted to remedy the situation by negotiating payment arrangements with the U.S. Department of Housing and Urban Development (HUD), only to shortly thereafter default on those arrangements. The village was now about $167,000 in arrears to HUD with interest payments, and about $339,874 in arrears with the City of Chicago Water Department. This financial crisis would continue to spiral completely out of control and haunt the village and its officials for decades to come.

Meanwhile, corruption in the village's water department was getting increased attention. Funds were simply not being accounted for, and it became obvious that a significant amount of money was disappearing from the collections of the water department. A large number of village residents had completely stopped paying their water bills amidst allegations of being charged for more than their actual consumption and usage by the village's water department. The money collected from the ever-shrinking pool of paying residents was suspected of being stolen by personnel in the department.

At a city council meeting held on February 13, 1979, Trustee Thomas moved the council to request that the federal government review operations of the village's water department. Trustee Ballentine seconded the motion; however, Mayor Smith refused to recognize both trustees and the motion. Irene Brodie, who was village clerk at the time, attempted to acknowledge Trustees Ballentine and Thomas, but as Mayor Smith had routinely done before, he abruptly attempted to silence her. Mayor Smith shouted, "Silence woman! I'll tell you when to speak." At times, Irene seemed nearly paralyzed by Mayor Smith's off-the-cuff and chauvinistic remarks. Mayor Smith could be very intimidating, even to the toughest of them. Standing over six feet tall and weighing in at over three hundred pounds, with a raspy, roaring voice, and not to mention, Mayor Smith seemed invincible wielding the mayor's gavel for three terms; Smith even began see himself as insuperable. It was as if Mayor Smith had not a clue that Irene, like himself, had been elected at-large, independently, by the residents of the Village of Robbins to serve them.

Ultimately, in spite of the roadblocks placed by Mayor Smith, a special undercover investigation was launched and an attempt was made to determine where the disappearing money was going that was draining the water department financially. The findings of the undercover investigation implicated one of the assistant clerks employed in the water department. Karen Rollins was implicated as one of the employees responsible for some of the money that was stolen. Sources close to the investigation and close to Karen Rollins tipped her off to the findings of the special investigation which caused her to flee the office just before law enforcement was able to move in and place her under arrest. Mrs. Rollins drove her car home and parked the vehicle in her garage where she left it running while inside, committing suicide. According to village officials and law enforcement authorities, Karen Rollins left behind a suicide note for her husband.

Once Mayor Smith had officially dismantled the village's police department, the Sheriff of Cook County was called in to maintain law and order in Robbins. Sheriff's deputies were assigned regular patrols in the village to provide safety and to protect the property of residents and businesses. This assistance from the Cook County Sheriff's Department didn't come free to the residents of Robbins.

The Village of Robbins paid out over $500,000 to the sheriff's department to cover its costs attributable to providing the Village of Robbins and its residents with around-the-clock police protection for nearly a year. This action drew widespread criticism of the village and Mayor Smith, and caused the Village of Robbins a considerable amount of embarrassment on a national scale.

The abolishment of the police department would ultimately have a devastating impact financially on the Village of Robbins. This action caused police officers, many of whom were residents of Robbins, to lose their jobs, and to be replaced by Cook County sheriff's deputies, who did not reside in the village. It cost village residents and taxpayers an exorbitant amount of money to pay the county sheriff's department for providing police services, services that could have been provided more efficiently had the village maintained its own trained and skilled force of officers. In addition, the Village of Robbins, Mayor Smith, and other high-ranking city officials were sued by police officers who alleged that they were wrongfully terminated. Some of those officers brought claims with merit and were awarded well over $500,000 in collective judgments. The Village of Robbins was also made to pay hundreds of thousands of dollars in legal fees associated with the ongoing litigation, which in a few cases progressed upwards to the U.S. Court of Appeals. The actions of Mayor Smith would have a devastating economic impact on the village for decades to come.

†

9

VILLAGE CLERK YEARS

"You may not control all the events that happen to you, but you can decide not to be reduced by them."

— *Dr. Maya Angelou*

Irene Brodie's success as a teacher earned her a high level of respect and applause in her hometown. Her achievements as an educator even caught the attention of then Robbins mayor, Earnest "Pete" Maxey. Mayor Maxey served as mayor for three consecutive terms, from 1957 to 1969. He was so impressed by Irene that he was determined to get her involved in government. He encouraged and motivated her to join him on his ticket for re-election as the candidate for village clerk in 1976. In 1977, Irene Brodie won election to the Office of Village Clerk of Robbins, Illinois and was sworn in to serve that same year. Irene entered the political arena after her husband, J.E. passed away. Mr. Brodie never became too engaged in politics because he did not want to mix politics with his responsibilities as an educator and school administrator.

Irene served as the clerk of the Village of Robbins for twelve years, the equivalent of three consecutive terms, and prior to becoming mayor of the village. She would successfully maintain her elective office of village clerk from 1977 to 1989. Mayor Maxey would serve as one of Irene's mentors in government. During that time, Irene was recognized for bringing a heightened level of professionalism and integrity to the clerk's office that permeated village government. Former Mayor Earnest "Pete" Maxey and Village Clerk

THE INHERITANCE OF A DREAM

Irene H. Brodie developed an excellent working and professional relationship and grew a close friendship. Irene not only served as clerk of the Village of Robbins, but she also became a trusted advisor and confidant of Mayor Maxey. Irene even stood firmly by Mayor Maxey when he faced criminal charges relating to the improper use of village funds, which ultimately resulted in him having to serve jail time. Irene Brodie assisted Mayor Maxey financially to help pay a debt he incurred resulting from his legal defense. Earnest "Pete" Maxey earned the infamous distinction of being the only mayor of the Village of Robbins to be incarcerated.

While serving in the capacity of village clerk, Irene immediately began to detect fraudulent activity conducted by some village employees. In some cases, village money was simply not being accounted for. The bookkeeping system was not accurate and consistent, and it was quite apparent that a significant amount of money was unaccounted for. The village's record keeping left a lot to be desired when Irene was sworn in as clerk. These deficiencies in the bookkeeping and record keeping of the village by some employees and officials seemed to serve as a green light for some to commit outright theft, and fraud involving village and taxpayers' funds. Irene was a virtuous woman; she was frugal and cleverly managed her finances. She had been married to a very financially successful man who was from a financially well-off family. Insiders knew that voters could trust her.

On occasion, political insiders went to Irene when they needed financial help, and oftentimes, she loaned them money. As time passed by, Irene became a little discontented because some of the associates and allies that she had supported financially, all but ignored their commitment to her and never paid back the money that she had loaned them. In a few cases, some even changed their political ideologies, withdrew political support and became her political adversaries.

As village clerk, Irene served with the administrations of three different mayors who preceded her in the mayor's office. She encountered some resistance from Mayor Richard Ballentine. Their relationship was not the best because Irene was recognized as an independent reformer with a high level of integrity, and this conflicted with the status quo, particularly with elected officials who were a part of the political machine holding power.

An already strained relationship between Irene and Mayor Ballentine took a turn for the worse when another independent, reform candidate was slated to run against a candidate backed by Mayor Ballentine, and caused an upset by defeating Mayor Ballentine's candidate by only three votes. State law required that the mayor, village clerk, and senior trustee sign the certification of the election results, thereby making the results legal. Mayor Ballentine and one of his supporters, Senior Trustee James Barnes, in a move of defiance, refused to affix their signatures to the certification of the 1983 general municipal election results. In addition, Mayor Ballentine instructed Irene to follow suit by refusing to sign the certification. However, upon obtaining legal counsel, Irene placed her signature on the certification of election results as was required of her position in accordance with state law. Her action angered Mayor Ballentine and caused such an uproar that the two would be staunch adversaries for a very long time. This matter would eventually advance to the courtroom, where ultimately, Mayor Ballentine and Senior Trustee Barnes were ordered to comply with state law, and to sign the election results certification or face removal from their office as well as jail time. Needless to say, both followed the court order and signed the election results certification. Consequently, they were both publically humiliated, and furious with Irene Brodie.

The professional relations between Mayor Ballentine, Village Clerk Brodie, and opposing members of the Village Board of Trustees had become so hostile, that on one occasion, guns were brandished in the council chambers during a council meeting. Mayor Ballentine drew stark criticism when he communicated to Irene with the use of derogatory and profane language, demanding that she "Shut up." During this tense encounter between Mayor Ballentine and Irene, the incident escalated to the point where Mayor Ballentine drew back his arm with a clinched fist as he approached Irene shouting obscene language at her. "You skinny ass bitch!" Mayor Ballentine shouted. Quickly, before he was able to land his fist on her, several members of the Village Board of Trustees rushed in to intervene, restraining Mayor Ballentine and preventing him from physically assaulting Irene. As recounted by members of the village board, this day represented one of the lowest moments in the history of village government. Mayor Ballentine's outrageous conduct not only added fuel to the fire, but it was very divisive and caused a permanent rift between members of the Village Board of Trustees and the Mayor.

It was Mayor Ballentine's unreasonable conduct that eventually led to his undoing as mayor. He routinely wore his pistol strapped visibly to his waist during council meetings. Members of the Village Board of Trustees and Irene believed that this was an overt attempt to intimidate his opponents and other sitting elected officials. In protest, Irene and several members of the Village Board of Trustees began to carry concealed firearms during council meetings, on occasion even displaying them. This conduct, reminiscent of the Wild, Wild West, would only lead to an increasingly hostile and strained relationship between Mayor Ballentine, Village Clerk Brodie, and members of the Village Board of Trustees.

†

10

LIFE OF THE PARTY

"I believe it is the responsibility of all to elevate the standards of the community through better government, education, aesthetics, and ethics."

—*Dr. Irene H. Brodie*

∽℧

The professional relationship between Mayor Richard Ballentine and Village Clerk Irene H. Brodie had become so badly damaged that it seemed irreparable. As the political leader of the New United Idea Party, Mayor Ballentine wielded a tremendous amount of influence among party loyalists. In retaliation, and in a surprising move against Irene Brodie, Mayor Ballentine expelled her from the party. She was devastated. Irene gracefully acknowledged her ouster from the party, but she felt alienated. She prided herself on the level of competence and professionalism she brought to the clerk's office, and not for her ability to play partisan politics.

Irene Brodie had served nearly two full terms as village clerk, and even her critics openly professed that her performance in that position was nothing short of admirable. Nevertheless, politics seemed to trump her performance, and the party's sitting leader, Mayor Ballentine, and other loyalists of the New United Idea Party despised her. Having served as village clerk for nearly eight years, alongside two mayors, Mayor Ballentine and his predecessor, Mayor Marion Smith, Irene was often openly treated with disrespect in her position. Mayors Ballentine and Smith, in many cases, simply refused to acknowledge and recognize the authority and independence vested by law in Irene Brodie and the Office of Village Clerk.

The Office of Village Clerk carries with it the responsibilities that are upheld by the laws of the State of Illinois. Traditionally, in terms of salary, Robbins' village clerk has been the second highest paid position in village government, second only to the salary paid to the village mayor. Irene recognized on repeated occasions that her male counterparts who held elective office often viewed the position of village clerk as a "girlie job." They often attempted to dictate to her how they wanted her to run the clerk's office, despite the fact that she was an independently elected official just as they had been. Irene was forced to tolerate this culture of disrespect that seemed to flourish under the administration of Mayor Marion Smith, and tensions came to a head under his successor, Mayor Richard Ballentine.

Soon, Irene would decide her intentions for seeking re-election to a third term to the Office of Village Clerk. She was now well past the midpoint of her second term, and had been ousted from the New United Idea Party by Mayor Ballentine. In response to the wave of corruption that permeated village government and the order of business of the political party holding power, there were a growing number of political independents who grew more outraged at the way local government was being administered in Robbins. Among the discontented were a growing number of independent politicians who openly and defiantly detested the Ballentine Administration and his party's political machine. This group was headed up by Tyrone Haymore, a local community activist turned political maverick.

Haymore embraced the integrity, style, and professionalism brought to the clerk's office by Irene Brodie. Haymore and Mrs. Brodie's acquaintance went back to the days when Mrs. Brodie served as Haymore's sixth grade teacher at Kellar Middle School. Now, Haymore had grown up to become a fine young man, making a name for himself by becoming politically active in the Robbins community. Even though Haymore was one of Mrs. Brodie's former sixth grade students, he had a few lessons in store for Irene Brodie in Robbins Politics 101.

Tyrone Haymore was a shrewd political insider who knew the nuts-and-bolts of how Robbins' political elite operated. He had a brilliant political mind and he had experience as a grassroots community organizer and activist, and he knew how to bring people together around issues of importance. As a member of the Village Board of Trustees, Mr. Haymore had witnessed firsthand the challenges faced by Irene on a continual basis. He also knew that Irene had been kicked out of the establishment's political party. Tyrone Haymore extended an olive branch to Mrs. Brodie and asked her to consider joining his political party and their newly organized efforts to bring reform to Robbins' village hall. Mr. Haymore had a keen sense for building coalitions around causes, and he had long recognized the power that Irene wielded as village clerk among many residents. She had been elected twice by decisive margins to serve as clerk, and she had very high performance ratings among voters. Haymore knew that if he could persuade Irene to align herself with his political party, together they could form a political alliance that would be unconquerable, even when up against the political machine of Incumbent Mayor Ballentine.

However, despite Irene's popularity as clerk, defeating the Ballentine endorsed candidate for village clerk would not be an easy task. At the time, the law allowed voters to vote for a "straight" ticket of candidates by simply punching one number on the election ballot. This meant that whoever Mayor Ballentine's choice for clerk would be, he or she could benefit from the incumbency of Mayor Ballentine. Irene had been expelled from Ballentine's political party. She was now on the outside, and in a sense on her own—a true independent. Mr. Haymore was aware that getting some members of his party to support Irene would prove challenging, since some leaders in the black community had labeled her as snobbish and bourgeois. He knew that this might prove difficult in a predominantly black town where most people identified themselves as common, working-class individuals. Irene, on the other hand, was viewed as being a highly educated, upper class woman. Irene was all too familiar with how some viewed her and she had reservations as to whether she would be embraced by members of the new political party. However, she was determined and as committed as ever to seek re-election to a third term as clerk of the Village of Robbins. In this regard, Irene accepted Haymore's invitation to consider wooing his organization's support for re-election to a third term as village clerk.

Haymore believed that if he could convince Irene to run for re-election for clerk on his party's ticket, her loyal supporters would greatly bolster his party's slated candidates' chances for victory. He believed that this wave of support could also lead to the defeat of Mayor Ballentine, whose popularity was steadily declining in the polls. The only potential obstacle that he faced was to convince his party regulars to support Irene, who was not a member of the party, over loyalists to the party who had already announced their intentions to run against Irene for her position. Florence Hawkins and James Kimbrough were two loyal members of the Better Government Party and the Concerned Taxpayers Party that had announced their candidacies for village clerk. To overcome this obstacle, Mr. Haymore convinced Irene to make a small monetary pledge for membership to the party. Mr. Haymore accepted her pledge and had a membership card signed by official party bosses and issued it to her. Now listed as a financial contributor to the party, and bearing in her possession an official party membership card, Irene was officially a member of the Better Government Party, and could attend and participate in the party's upcoming political convention.

Meanwhile, Tyrone Haymore worked behind the scenes, convincing party bosses, Eugene Cook and Ben Harvey, to embrace and support Irene as their choice for clerk as a way to significantly attract new voters to the party. In fact, polling indicated that Irene's popularity among likely voters surpassed not only that of the opposing party's choice for clerk, but also that of the Incumbent Mayor Richard Ballentine. Using Mayor Ballentine's harsh treatment of Irene as a political issue seemed to resonate with potential voters, especially women. Voters who may have otherwise supported Mayor Ballentine's opposing party, were now willing to crossover in support of the incumbent clerk, Irene Brodie. After considerable thought, party leaders sided with Tyrone Haymore and embraced Irene's effort to seek re-election with the endorsement of the Better Government Party. They acknowledged that Irene's loyal supporters could lead to a groundswell of support for the party. This strategy, masterminded by Haymore, also seemed to provide a clever way of rallying voters in support of Irene, and in opposition to Mayor Ballentine and his hand-picked choice to replace her as village clerk. Mayor Ballentine's mistreatment and ousting of Irene Brodie would ultimately become his downfall and serve as a reason for his opponents to rally against his re-election.

With the election drawing closer, Eugene Cook, Ben Harvey, Tyrone Haymore, and other Better Government Party leaders convened their political convention in the gymnasium of Thomas J. Kellar Middle School. Much to the surprise of many delegates, two highly regarded party operatives, Haymore allies, and party loyalists, Ruby Husband and Flournoy "Coolbreeze" Clemons, nominated Irene H. Brodie for village clerk on the floor of the convention against two party insiders, James Kimbrough and Florence Hawkins. To the surprise of many, Irene H. Brodie won the party's nomination for village clerk. The Better Government Party was now obligated to support her as its nominee, and the other candidates that comprised the party's ticket. Incumbent Village Clerk Irene Brodie, with her proven track record and popularity among voters, had transcended party lines, making her what many party leaders described as the "Life of the Party." The candidacy of Irene H. Brodie for re-election as village clerk galvanized voters around the issues of honesty and integrity, and significantly bolstered support for the Better Government Party and its candidate for mayor, John W. Hamilton. On Election Day, when the votes were tallied, this wave of new support garnered by Irene for the Better Government Party translated into the defeat of Mayor Richard Ballentine by Mayor-Elect John Hamilton. Irene H. Brodie, the Better Government Party's choice for village clerk won with overwhelming support. In addition, three new trustees were elected to serve as well—Willie Carter, Richard Williams, and Florence Hawkins were all slated by the Better Government Party.

†

Irene's parents, Ira and Ressie Hale (circa 1950).

Irene (far right, rear) joins her parents, Ira and Ressie, (seated, left to right) and two of her sisters, Evelyn, (2nd from right) and her youngest sister Bertha (far right), in a family photo. Irene's eldest sister, Ethel, is pictured in lower left photo (circa 1951).

Mr. and Mrs. Brodie (above-left) are joined
by friends Mr. and Mrs. Kimbell for an awards
dinner at the former Chuck Cavallini's Restaurant in Midlothian, Illinois, hosted
by the Illinois Education School Principals Association (IESPA) (circa 1963).
Mr. Brodie was Principal of Eisenhower High School (Southeast Campus) and
Mrs. Brodie was Assistant Principal of Turner Elementary School in Robbins,
Illinois. Mr. and Mrs. Brodies' professional school photos are inset bottom right.

Irene stands outside her parents' home in Missouri, holding her
infant daughter, Jeraye. Standing alongside them is her mother, Ressie.
Inset: Jeraye smiles and stands confidently at 2 years old (circa 1959).

Irene H. Brodie (front row, far right) poses with her 6th Grade Class at Kellar Grade School for their official class photo (1962).

Irene (inset) joins fellow members of Kappa Delta Pi International Honor Society for an honorary dinner at the Conrad Hilton Hotel in downtown Chicago (1961).

Jeraye takes time away
from her academic studies
to practice playing her
organ at the family home
in Robbins (circa 1970).

Irene Brodie provides instruction
to one of her students in the
communications lab at Moraine
Valley Community College (circa
1971).

Irene graduates from the University of Chicago, receiving a Master of Science degree in Education (1968). Photo taken by Jeraye Brodie.

It's official! Dr. Brodie graduates and receives her Doctoral Degree in Education from Nova Southeast University located in Ft. Lauderdale, Florida (1996).

Dean Brodie, shown with
colleague Dr. William
Mueller, offers advice to a
student at Moraine Valley
Community College (2001).

Doors are open at the Dr. Irene
H. Brodie Academic Skills Center
at Moraine Valley Community
College, which provides assistance
to students needing to improve
their basic academic skills.

"Punch 10 and Win!" was the slogan used by Unity Party candidates, including mayoral candidate Dr. Irene H. Brodie. Robbins' voters responded in the affirmative, electing Dr. Brodie as the first female mayor in the history of the village. Pictured is a photo of the candidates' campaign poster (1989).

The People's Choice: Mayor-Elect Irene H. Brodie (2nd from left) who headed the Unity Party's ticket as its mayoral candidate, is congratulated on her victory. Alongside her, Tyrone Haymore (left) Unity Party founder and newly elected village clerk, newly elected Village Board Trustees, Willie Carter (center), Palma James (2nd from right), and Richard Williams (far right) (1989).

She's Official! Mayor Brodie's
official photo as the Mayor of
the Village of Robbins, Illinois.

Mayor Brodie (2nd from left) takes a rare photo op with three of four of her
mayoral predecessors. Former Mayor Earnest Maxey, Sr. (left), Former Mayor
Marion "Big Man" Smith (2nd from right) and former Mayor John Hamilton
(right). Former Mayor Richard Ballentine was not present for photo op (1990).

Then-Illinois State Senator Barack Obama (3rd from left) visits Moraine Valley Community College; joining him are, left to right, college President Dr. Vernon Crawley, Diane Viverito, Director of International Student Affairs, Illinois State Senator Louis Viverito, Dr. Irene H. Brodie, and Illinois State Senate President Emil Jones, Sr. (circa 1998)

Then-Illinois state Senator Barack Obama (2nd from right) visits Robbins' Community Center; joining him are Robbins Mayor Brodie (front, center), Congressman Danny K. Davis (left), Illinois Senate President Emil Jones, Sr. (far right) and Chicago Alderman William Beavers (behind Mayor Brodie) (circa 1997).

Mayor Brodie (center) joined by village board trustees, executives of Foster-Wheeler, Inc., and Reading Energy Corp. break ground for the construction of the $300 million waste-to-energy facility in Robbins (1994).

The iconic landmark Robbins water tower rises high above the north end of the village, welcoming residents and visitors as they enter Robbins. In the background is the once vibrant waste-to-energy facility.

Mayor Brodie is joined by Richard M. Daley, Mayor of Chicago. Both mayors served six consecutive four-year terms as mayor of their respective municipalities, earning each the distinction of being the longest serving mayor in the history of their municipalities (circa 2002).

Mayor Brodie enjoys an evening on the town with Cook County Commissioner, and nationally-acclaimed musician and singer, Jerry "Ice-Man" Butler (circa 2001).

Mayor Brodie shares a moment with one of her strongest political allies, the Cook County Board President John H. Stroger. President Stroger played a pivotal role in bringing better healthcare to the community by approving the construction of the Cook County Medical Clinic in Robbins (2000).

Mayor Brodie (right) joins in the victory celebration of the election of Carol Moseley-Braun (center) to the United States Senate. Joining them is Mayor Brodie's dear friend, Dr. William Jackson (left) (1998).

Mayor Brodie (center) is joined by Illinois Governor-Elect Rod Blagojevich (left) and Illinois state Senator-Elect Reverend James Meeks (2002).

Mayor Brodie (right) is joined by then-Illinois Attorney General Roland Burris. Years later, Burris was appointed to fill the U.S. Senate seat vacated by President Barack Obama (1992).

Mayor Brodie (center) is accompanied by the "Shaw Brothers." William Shaw (left), mayor of Dolton, Illinois, and Illinois state senator, and Robert Shaw (right) former Chicago Alderman, and former Cook County Tax Appeals Board member. The Shaw twins proved to be two of Mayor Brodie's strongest political allies (circa 1994).

Mayor Brodie is congratulated by President William "Bill" Clinton. She served on President Clinton's Environmental Think-Tank Group (circa 1995).

Mayor Brodie (2nd from left) is joined by Congressman Jesse Jackson, Jr. (left), Mayor Evans Miller of Markham, Illinois (2nd from right), and Jesse Louis Jackson, Sr. (right) (circa 1994).

Mayor Brodie visits the Taj Mahal while vacationing in Bombay (Mumbai) India.

Mayor Brodie meets with a Kenyan government official to discuss accomplishments made by her administration relating to environmental issues in the United States.

Dr. Irene Brodie has been a devout member of Great Hope M.B. Church since moving to Robbins in the mid-1950s. She was a most loyal supporter of Pastor W. L. Cook and one of Great Hope's largest financial contributors.

11

LADY B

"It really wasn't my decision; it was my direction that was given to me spiritually. My daughter used to always say to me, 'Mom, when I finish my bachelor's degree, I'm going to come back and work with Robbins. Somebody's got to get out there and do it.' Those words came back to me. There was something that God wanted me to do."

—*Dr. Irene H. Brodie*

The descendant of parents born and raised in the South during the Jim Crow Era; parents who were forced by state law to pay a poll tax in order to exercise their right to vote, Dr. Irene H Brodie won election to the Office of Mayor of Robbins, Illinois. She was the first woman to serve in that capacity.

By law, the Village of Robbins Board of Trustees is responsible for executing certain governing actions. Actions taken by the board can take the form of ordinances and resolutions, which require the approval of the mayor, and legal publication where required by law. An ordinance is generally a legislative act of the Board of Trustees to adopt laws and regulations for the village. A resolution is generally a formal statement of decision, opinion, or determination of policy adopted by the board to exercise ministerial functions. Appointments to boards and commissions are the responsibility of the mayor with the advice and consent of the Board of Trustees. A motion is generally a procedural action in a board meeting put forth in order to formally consider ordinances or resolutions, file reports, or request that certain action be taken by the administration. A motion must be seconded, and barring certain exceptions, majority approval is required.

THE INHERITANCE OF A DREAM

With her election as the first female mayor of the Village of Robbins, Dr. Irene H. Brodie was recognized as part of an elite club, or sisterhood, and became known as "Lady B." In the year 1989, several municipalities located in the South Suburbs of Chicago held their city-wide elections, and two other suburban communities were recognized for electing their first African-American female mayor in the history of their respective towns. The voters of Ford Heights, Illinois, elected Gloria Bryant as mayor, and in the Village of Phoenix, Illinois, January Belmont was elected mayor, in addition to Robbins mayor, Dr. Irene Brodie's ascension. In the Village of Robbins, several prior village presidents had opted to assume the title of "Mayor," even though the legal description was technically "Village President," until legally changed to "Mayor" under Mayor Brodie's Administration. The national media, including Chicago based Tribune-owned station WGN-TV, covered the historic achievements accomplished by these three mayors in the Chicago Southland. In her report, WGN-Channel 9 reporter Merri Dee dubbed these three ladies the "Lady Bs," because all of their last names—Belmont, Bryant and Brodie—each began with the letter "B." From that day forward, Mayor Brodie also became affectionately known as "Lady B."

Village Clerk Brodie had developed such a reputation for bringing high, professional standards and integrity to the clerk's office that some of her colleagues in municipal government, along with community leaders, encouraged her to seek the Office of Mayor. Irene expressed appreciation to all those who implored her to run for mayor, however, she adamantly declined their invitations, initially.

At the time, Irene was still grieving from the untimely death of her daughter, Jeraye, and having numerous responsibilities as not only the Village Clerk, but also Dean of Educational Development at Moraine Valley Community College. Among those who pledged support for Irene to run for mayor was one of her political mentors, former Mayor Earnest "Pete" Maxey. Former Mayor Maxey confided in Irene that he thought she would make an excellent mayor, and urged her to pray and follow God's direction when making her final decision.

Community and political activists stepped up their political campaign to elect a new mayor by creating a new political party, the Unity Party. In 1988, Tyrone Haymore, then a village trustee, and an outspoken critic of the sitting mayor, John W. Hamilton, founded the new party. Both Trustee Haymore and then-mayor, John Hamilton, were members of the Better Government Party. Due to a wave of corruption that had permeated Mayor Hamilton's Administration, opposition to his re-election began to mount quickly.

Even some of the political insiders that were once a vital part of the Hamilton Camp, including Dr. Irene Brodie and Trustee Haymore, were preparing to jump ship and rally against Mayor Hamilton's re-election. Trustee Haymore accused Mayor Hamilton of attempting to bribe him by offering him a portion of $30,000, village money stemming from proceeds received from a municipal agreement with a business formerly known as TCI, a local cable operator doing business with the Village of Robbins, in exchange for Trustee Haymore turning a blind eye and helping to conceal inappropriate expenditures allegedly made by Mayor Hamilton and members of his administration. As a ranking member of the Village Board of Trustees, Haymore served as chairman of the Finance Committee. Serving in that capacity, he had clear insight into nearly every expenditure that Mayor Hamilton and his administration had made. Haymore was also privy to every agreement made and any debt incurred by the village.

Trustee Haymore presented his concerns of corruption and financial improprieties to the leadership of the Better Government Party, which promised a swift and thorough investigation of Mayor Hamilton and the alleged conduct. As anticipated by Haymore, ultimately the party's brass was unwilling to side with Haymore and go against its political standard-bearer, Mayor Hamilton. The Better Government Party announced that they found absolutely no evidence of wrongdoing relating to any financial transactions involving village money expended by Mayor Hamilton or any members of his staff. The Better Government Party also made it clear that its members had every intention to support Mayor Hamilton in his upcoming bid for re-election.

The Village of Robbins' financial condition continued to worsen, pushing the village to the brink of bankruptcy. Haymore completely lost faith in Mayor Hamilton and his administration, and eventually resigned from his position as Mayor pro tempore. For about two years, Haymore abstained from actively participating in party politics and focused his energies on defeating Mayor Hamilton for re-election.

This was a critical time in the history of Robbins, Illinois. The village was in such bad financial shape that there was talk about the village filing for bankruptcy protection, being dissolved as a municipality or possibly being annexed by one of its neighboring towns. There was much doubt that the village would be able to continue operating as an independent municipality. This grave condition seemed to greatly motivate political activists and business and community leaders to search even harder for a qualified candidate that could help bail Robbins out and provide the village with a road map to a brighter future. Dr. Irene Brodie was reluctant to run for mayor because of her experience as village clerk for over ten years. Her participation in the party politics of the village had convinced her that Robbins' political climate was male-dominated. She did not think that would change anytime soon. Dr.

Brodie also recognized that she was not favored by some political insiders who rarely missed an opportunity to portray her as "bourgeoisie."

There were some who still harbored ill feelings for Irene stemming back from her feud with former Mayor Ballentine. Those wounds ran very deep. Years later, even after residents voted Mayor Ballentine out of office and replaced him with a new mayor, John Hamilton, bad feelings persisted between Ballentine's supporters, who had expelled Irene from the party, and her supporters. Dr. Brodie was also mindful of the fact that only once in the history of the Village of Robbins had a woman run for the highest office.

In 1952, Elinor Robinson White, a loyalist of and speechwriter for Marcus Garvey, ran an unsuccessful campaign for mayor against Theodore Hendricks. Elinor Robinson White was the first woman to be elected clerk of the Village of Robbins. White served as village clerk from 1949 through 1953. In 1952, while holding the office of village clerk, she unsuccessfully challenged Hendricks for the office of mayor. Hendricks won the election by a wide margin. Irene Brodie knew that breaking the glass ceiling put in place by the "Old Boys Network" and its political party, would certainly not be an easy accomplishment. Although Irene was intrigued by the possibility of running for the village's highest office, she reasoned that now probably would not be the best time for such a bold and daring undertaking.

After several unsuccessful attempts to persuade Dr. Brodie to run as a candidate for mayor, suddenly, she began to show a newly sparked interest. She expressed that her change in position was attributed to her passion for helping youth, particularly those who aspired to improve their education, but would be hindered from doing so because of financial limitations. She believed that becoming mayor would enable her to have a positive impact on the lives of village residents and also have a more powerful platform to help youngsters in the community improve their education by seeking a higher level of learning through attending college. Dr. Irene H. Brodie was a staunch advocate of achieving academic excellence. She often expressed that a good education is the key to a productive and prosperous life. Dr. Brodie expressed that her daughter's dream inspired and called her to action.

After having successfully served twelve years as the clerk of the Village of Robbins, Irene Brodie had earned the loyal support of residents, community leaders, and other local government officials. She had crossed party lines in her last re-election for clerk, and she increased her support among new voters. It was this groundswell of loyal and unwavering support from grassroots organizations and community leaders that would propel Irene into her next role in government. An effort to draft Irene Brodie for mayor was organized and quickly began to flourish.

The Unity Party slated a field of candidates to run on their party ticket in the 1989 Robbins Municipal Election. Dr. Irene H. Brodie headed the ticket as the party's choice for mayor. Tyrone Haymore received the party's nomination for village clerk. Richard Williams, Willie Carter, and Palma L. James were all slated by the party for positions on the Village Board of Trustees. Palma L. James, who was among those nominated for village board trustee, was the only other woman on the party's ticket besides Irene.

Irene gives the credit for her decision to run for mayor to her spiritual being. "It really wasn't my decision; it was my direction that was given to me spiritually. My daughter used to always say to me, 'Mom, when I finish my bachelor's degree, I'm going to come back and work with Robbins. Somebody's got to get out there and do it.' " Those words came back to me. There was something that God wanted me to do. I was discouraged with the progress of our town and my position was that I've been here twelve years and I served [alongside] three different mayors. I've seen nothing happening that would make me think my position here [as village clerk] is making a difference."

During the mayoral campaign, a village financial crisis had become a political issue for opposing parties. A check for $49,000 in back taxes sent to the Internal Revenue Service in December 1988 was returned to the village because there was not enough money in the village payroll account to cover the check. According to Trustee Hearthel Johnson, who served as the Robbins Board of Trustees' Finance Committee Chairman, the village submitted the check to the IRS, but "it bounced because we were one hundred dollars short in the account." Johnson stated that the necessary funds were deposited and a second check was issued, but he blamed Irene for not mailing the check to the IRS, and placing a void on the check instead. "That is not true," Irene responded. "I cannot void the check. I am not authorized to void the checks." Irene asserted that the false allegations stemmed from Johnson's attempt to keep Mayor John Hamilton in office. "This is just one way they [Hamilton and his supporters] are trying to make me look bad in the election," Irene stated. Mayor Hamilton alleged that the confusion over the checks resulted in the IRS placing a levy against several of the village's banking accounts, leaving only one dollar in each account.

Dr. Brodie also stated, "The mayor is looking for a cause to keep me out of the mayoral race, and if my team wins, Johnson would be the only carry-over from Hamilton's party. Trustee Johnson knows I never voided the check and I would never interfere with the IRS." Irene went even further and accused Mayor Hamilton of squandering village money and paying his favorite employees extra money.

Under Illinois law, small municipalities are not required to participate in the two-party political system that is normally identified with national elections. As a result, these smaller municipalities do not participate in political primaries. This makes for an election process that is considerably less expensive.

When Tyrone Haymore founded the Unity Party in 1988, and Dr. Brodie agreed to head the party's ticket as its choice for mayor against Incumbent Mayor John Hamilton, Tyrone Haymore and Dr. Brodie were instrumental in developing the party's platform, focusing on economic development and reform for the Village of Robbins. With three successful terms as village clerk to her credit, and still riding a wave of popularity in the political polls among potential voters, Irene H. Brodie had emerged as a favorite in the race for mayor.

Subsequent to his election as village clerk, Haymore was also elected by members of the Black Elected Officials of Illinois (BEOI) to serve as treasurer of the organization. Initially, the BEOI was founded and organized by Roland Burris, then-comptroller of the State of Illinois. The organization was first established as the Black Elected Officials of Cook County, and was renamed as membership rapidly grew to include prominent officials throughout the entire state. Subsequently as Mayor of Robbins, Dr. Brodie joined Chicago Mayor Harold Washington as a member of the Black Elected Officials of Illinois, and Dr. Brodie was elected by BEOI members to serve as secretary of the organization.

"Punch Ten and Win," was the slogan shouted by Dr. Brodie, Haymore, Carter, James, Williams, and the other slated candidates of the Unity Party as they campaigned throughout the village. In 1989, election law allowed voters to vote for a slate of candidates with the same political party affiliation by simply casting a "straight party vote." However, years later, election law was changed, banning straight party voting for candidates. Voters were then required to cast separate and individual votes for their choice of candidates, regardless of their party affiliation. Once this new law was put into effect, it made it much more difficult for a lesser desired candidate to win on the coat tails of popular candidates, simply due to a similarity in political party affiliation. It empowered voters with the ability to choose each individual candidate seeking elective office.

Riding a wave of popularity and support among voters based on her stellar performance as village clerk, and coupled with her pledge to eradicate corruption in city government, Dr. Brodie was victorious in her campaign for mayor. After finishing first in a grueling campaign, Dr. Brodie realized her toughest days were still ahead.

Once elected mayor, and taking on the responsibilities of the Office of Mayor, Dr. Brodie had to immediately focus on getting Robbins' financial house in order. When she took office, the city's phone bill was five months past due, there was an IRS lien on village accounts, and no one on the municipal payroll had seen a paycheck in over a month.

Much to the surprise of her political adversaries, Mayor Brodie did not "clean house" upon assuming the Office of Mayor. She did not execute mass firings of city department heads and employees who were performing satisfactorily in their respective positions. Some expected her to immediately terminate many employees stemming over from Mayor Hamilton's Administration. Instead, Mayor Brodie offered many city department heads and employees an olive branch with an opportunity to demonstrate their ability to improve their performance and execute her agenda in moving the village forward.

A few months after taking office, Mayor Brodie participated in her first ribbon-cutting ceremony, marking the opening of the Kedzie Avenue Bridge. This was a construction project spearheaded by Cook County government and initiated under former Mayor John Hamilton's Administration. The Bridge connected and extended Kedzie Avenue at Claire Boulevard to 142nd Street in neighboring Midlothian. The road construction provided a major thoroughfare that linked the City of Chicago to the South Suburbs, running right through the heart of Robbins.

12

BLIND JUSTICE

"What is permissible is not always honorable."

—*Marcus Tullius Cicero*

During her time in office, Mayor Brodie was faced with a growing number of lawsuits against the village. Most of the lawsuits were claims involving the actions of the village's police department. Over ninety-five percent of the lawsuits targeting the village included allegations of police brutality or some form of police misconduct.

One notable case was *William Renji v. Village of Robbins, Robbins Police Department, et al.* A white motorist and non-resident of the village was driving through the community and made a stop in the Willett Public Housing Project. Members of the Robbins Police Department suspected that he was involved in illegal activity and established just cause to pursue the alleged offender. Police officers claimed the suspect was engaging in a drug deal and instructed the suspect to freeze. According to police, the suspect refused to halt, and instead reached for an item that they believed to be a gun. Robbins police officers shot the suspect, causing him to sustain injuries that left him permanently paralyzed from the neck down.

Mr. Renji's attorney filed a lawsuit against the Village of Robbins and its police department. As an internal police investigation ensued, it was initially determined that the responding Robbins police officers had acted properly; they followed all departmental rules and they had established that they had probable cause to pursue the suspect. According to village officials, the officer was able to prove that he acted justifiably and in accordance with departmental guidelines and procedures authorizing the use of his firearm. It seemed as if this lawsuit would be an open and shut case; at least, that is what village officials and their attorneys believed.

In a legal maneuver made by the plaintiff's attorney, opposing counsel subpoenaed all official records dating back as far as twenty years prior to the incident. The opposing counsel focused on ordinances and resolutions that were approved by the Village Board of Trustees and the mayor. When sifting through these official records, attorneys representing the plaintiff observed that back in 1978, former Robbins Mayor Marion Smith, had abolished the entire police department.

A year after abolishing the department, Mayor Smith restructured the police department, renaming it the Robbins Department of Public Safety. He hired all new officers. The opposing counsel observed that Mayor Smith and the Robbins Village Board of Trustees had failed to pass an ordinance legally re-establishing the village's police department. The plaintiff's attorney had now unearthed evidence that the Robbins "Public Safety Department" was not legally and duly organized. Therefore, Robbins police officers were not legally authorized to conduct any police functions, and certainly not authorized to apply deadly force against the plaintiff that resulted in his injuries, leaving him paralyzed for the remainder of his life. Eventually, the Village of Robbins lost the lawsuit, and the plaintiff was awarded $1 million.

Already in dire financial condition, the Village of Robbins now had a $1 million verdict pending against it, and no money to pay it. Ultimately, the court approved a payment plan that allowed the Village of Robbins to pay Mr. Renji approximately $50,000 annually for twenty years. In the year 2012, according to village officials, after twenty years of struggling to meet those annual payments, the Village of Robbins finally fulfilled its obligation under court order by completely paying the monetary judgment awarded to the plaintiff.

†

13

THE BURNER WARS

"I keep running. In college I was a sprinter. I did the seventy-five yard dash. Now, it seems I'm doing a marathon."

—*Dr. Irene H. Brodie*

In the State of Illinois, different developers were planning to build as many as twenty-five incinerators (waste-to-energy facilities) to burn waste. Approximately twenty-five percent of the incinerators were expected to be concentrated in the South and Southwest Suburbs. Ford Heights, Illinois constructed an incinerator to burn and recycle tires. McCook, Illinois had a wood burning incinerator, and Robbins and Summit, Illinois would have incinerators burn and recycle garbage. Harvey, Illinois was expected to have an incinerator with a capacity to burn an anticipated forty-eight tons of medical waste per day.

These incinerators were expected to receive a reasonable federal subsidy to operate. In spite of this, an overwhelming majority of states in the country rejected allowing incinerators to operate in their own state. Illinois had easily become the most attractive state for developers of incinerators because of the creation of the Retail Rate Law. The Retail Rate Law allows for an incinerator company to burn garbage, and in the process, produce electricity. The company could then sell the electricity to the local power company which, according to federal guidelines, would be required to purchase the electricity. Since the federal government would offer the incinerator company a subsidy, this would boost the price of electricity that the local power company must pay the incinerator company to purchase its output of electricity. The Retail Rate Law should be a win-win situation for all involved.

THE INHERITANCE OF A DREAM

The Illinois Retail Rate Law offered incinerator companies a subsidy that would significantly increase their profit margins. In fact, the Retail Rate Law would make the difference between an incinerator operator turning a significant profit or operating at a complete loss. The Robbins incinerator was by some estimates expected to claim $15 million in state subsidized payments every year for twenty years. That is an estimated $300 million. The local electric company, Commonwealth Edison, in the case of the Robbins incinerator, would receive a tax break in the amount of the difference between the actual cost to produce the electricity and the premium cost that it would be required to pay the incinerator as a result of the subsidies.

Without this subsidy provided by the Retail Rate Law, the operators of the Robbins incinerator, Foster-Wheeler of Illinois and Reading Energy Company of Pennsylvania, would not make a profit. It was expected that the State of Illinois would eventually get repaid the money to subsidize the incinerators. The subsidy would also be considered a no-interest loan to the incinerator developers. After twenty years of operating, the incinerators were expected to start repaying the money. However, critics of the Retail Rate Law asserted that repayment of the subsidies was impractical, because after twenty years the incinerators would be too old, too obsolete, and too inefficient. They thought that it would be easier for the incinerator company to simply walk away in the face of owing the state over $300 million.

Initially, when the Retail Rate Law was first passed, it was touted as being good for the environment. The State of Illinois was expected to run out of landfill space to bury garbage, so legislative leaders professed that incinerators were the next best option.

In 1989, the Village of Robbins began planning a waste management complex with a recycling and fuel processing facility and a 1,600 tons-per-day (TPD) fluidized bed waste combustion plant. Construction commenced on the project in the fall of 1994 after several hurdles involving its applications for permits to build, and after several surrounding communities agreed to send their waste to the plant.

Mayor Irene Brodie had been a strong supporter of the project since its inception. She believed that the new waste-to-energy facility would bring economic benefits to her community while safely fulfilling an important public health service. In May 1993, Mayor Brodie stated in a letter to the NAACP,

"For the past ten years I have been at the forefront of an effort to bring economic development to our village through environmental improvements to the area south of Chicago. We can accomplish these goals by the development of a modern recycling and trash-to-energy facility."

Many of the residents of Robbins, the majority of whom are African-American, and many of whom live below the national poverty line, joined Mayor Brodie in supporting the project. In an April 1993 referendum, 80 percent of the residents voted in favor of the waste-to-energy project, convinced that it would significantly improve their community.

The waste-to-energy project was expected to create 600 construction jobs for a three-year period and a minimum of eighty permanent jobs once the plant became operational in 1997. More than half of these jobs were expected to be filled by residents of Robbins. The waste-to-energy project was also expected to spark significant economic development in the village. With very little business or industry in the village and with an almost exclusively residential tax base, the village, with a current population of slightly less than 7,000 people, was operating on the brink of bankruptcy. The waste-to-energy plant was expected to boost the village's existing tax base by seventy percent. Robbins would also benefit as the facility's host community, with free trash disposal, as well as special revenues set aside for off-site economic development projects within the village. For instance, Seaway Bank, one of the largest African-American owned banks in the nation, had planned to open a branch in the village.

Facilities that recover energy value from combustion of solid waste have commonly been called resource recovery or waste-to-energy facilities. Most of the time, the energy and material recovery that occurs at these facilities is overlooked, since their primary function is to serve as waste disposal facilities. The benefit of using local, renewable fuel would help to reduce dependence upon oil and to conserve such nonrenewable fuels. On average, most waste-to-energy plants generated between 500 and 600-kilowatt hours (kWh) of electricity for each ton of trash they burned. Since the industry was still relatively young, efficiencies were improving each year, making for an even greater level of productivity. Most waste-to-energy plants also recovered materials for recycling, helping boost the community's recycling rate beyond what curbside and drop-off programs could achieve. The materials recovered were usually ferrous and nonferrous metals captured from the ash after combustion. Some plants recovered metals and other recyclables both pre- and post-combustion.

The Robbins incinerator targeted 25 percent recovery from the municipal solid waste (MSW) it received, and most of the 400 tons per day that it expected to process would represent materials outside of the residential waste stream collected at curbside. Ferrous scrap, tin and aluminum cans, compostable materials, glass, rock, and grit as a whole would add to recovery levels from the community's curbside program.

THE INHERITANCE OF A DREAM

Dr. Brodie's determination to secure the waste-to-energy facility for the Village of Robbins earned her quite a reputation as the village's mayor, and put her at odds with several neighboring towns and their residents who opposed Robbins being the location of the incinerator. Perhaps the most prominent of those who opposed the incinerator being located in Robbins, was Illinois' Second Congressional District representative, Congressman Jesse Jackson, Jr., as well as his father, the Reverend Jesse L. Jackson. Both of the Jacksons stood in staunch opposition to Mayor Brodie's efforts to secure this modern waste-to-energy facility for the Village of Robbins.

Mayor Brodie contended that this type of facility was just what the village needed in order to create an economic stimulus. On the other hand, the Jacksons argued that the facility posed significant health risks for the residents of Robbins and that the facility would be bad for the environment. Both Jacksons were so vocal in their opposition to Mayor Brodie and the village's attempt to build such a facility, that they went as far as to organize and demonstrate in order to block Mayor Brodie and the village from obtaining the necessary approval needed to attract and secure the facility. Since the Village of Robbins was at the time located within the legal boundaries of the Second Congressional District in Illinois, represented by Congressman Jackson, he wielded a considerable amount of influence in the village as well as in neighboring towns, particularly those that were adamantly opposed to Mayor Brodie and the Village of Robbins hosting the waste-to energy facility.

Mayor Brodie's hands were already full, waging an intense battle to secure the waste-to-energy project for the village, when another issue arose that threatened to undermine and impede her efforts. It was revealed that a village board trustee, Willie Hodges, was attempting to shake down project developers for money in exchange for his vote to approve the construction of the waste-to-energy facility in Robbins. Project developers had informed sources close to Mayor Brodie of Trustee Hodges' demand. Mayor Brodie immediately denounced Trustee Hodges' conduct and demanded that he immediately issue a full apology to the project developers or face being kicked out of their political party. Of course, being fully exposed, Trustee Hodges followed the mayor's advice. While maintaining his support of the project, he immediately retracted his request and ceased his efforts to demand money from developers in exchange for an affirmative vote.

Shortly thereafter, Mayor Brodie found herself presiding over city council meetings with the council chambers full to capacity and overflowing with protestors primarily comprised of residents from nearby towns and cities that had come to protest the village's efforts to gain approval to build the incinerator.

Most of the organized opposition to the incinerator claimed to object on the basis that the facility would be environmentally unsafe and would pose health risks to not only the residents of Robbins, but to residents of all the neighboring towns as well. Mayor Brodie and other village officials dismissed these claims, citing that all environmental studies that had been performed indicated otherwise and that the facility would be among the safest in the nation. They contended that the organized protests that were instigated, in part by the Jacksons, Jesse Jr. and Jesse Sr., were simply an attempt to deprive Robbins of the economic stimulus that the Village had worked so diligently for and that it so badly needed.

It appeared that Congressman Jesse Jackson was motivated by political reasons to block Robbins from obtaining the incinerator. He added insult to injury, given the fact that Mayor Brodie and her constituents, the residents of Robbins, were also constituents of his. Congressman Jackson had chosen to align himself with the so called "environmentalists" in an effort to defeat the village's attempt to win its bid for the incinerator. Of course, those in the village who knew better realized that Congressman Jackson was simply practicing his brand of politics. He had chosen to favor opponents of the incinerator, particularly those from white communities surrounding Robbins who were staunchly opposed to the incinerator being located in Robbins.

Congressman Jackson was clearly blocking Robbins' quest for economic growth as a way of building up political capital with some of his white constituents, some of whom actually wanted to have the incinerator located in their communities so that they could reap the economic benefits instead of the residents of Robbins. Congressman Jackson played right into their hands, joined by his father, Reverend Jackson, who seemed to be motivated by personal gain and publicity. The Jacksons and their followers' presence escalated to such a point that it was believed that Congressman Jackson and his father had summoned some of their constituents and supporters from Chicago to come to Robbins and join in on protests against Mayor Brodie and the village's efforts. Ultimately, the residents of the Village of Robbins and Mayor Brodie would prevail in their efforts to land the incinerator, but only after an intense ten-year long battle. After relentless effort by the people of Robbins, administrators, and officials of the village, Robbins was granted permission and issued permits to build the incinerator. At last, the best interests of the residents of the village had finally prevailed.

Perhaps no other issue that had arisen during Mayor Brodie's tenure tested her leadership, determination, and resolve more than her commitment to secure the waste-to-energy facility for the Village of Robbins.

THE INHERITANCE OF A DREAM

Environmentalists and other critics in and outside of the village also organized against Mayor Brodie and the Village of Robbins' efforts to build and operate a garbage-burning incinerator. Without the generous subsidy, the incinerators would contribute far less money to their host communities.

Governor Jim Edgar reviewed legislation passed by the Illinois General Assembly in January 1996 that would end the Retail Rate Law. Edgar's anticipated approval of the bill threatened to have a devastating impact on the Robbins incinerator and the people of the Village of Robbins. Mayor Brodie and the Village of Robbins pleaded with Governor Jim Edgar to keep the tax subsidy for the Robbins incinerator because the construction project was well underway. Governor Edgar suggested, in response, that he planned to approve a full repeal of the law that would take the subsidy away from them.

"Those bonds [issued to finance the Robbins incinerator] sold at a very high premium because they were viewed as a risk," Edgar said. "I think those people who went out there knew there was always the possibility that this was something that could be changed because it was controversial."

In an interview with the *Chicago Tribune*, Mayor Brodie stated,

> "Communities like mine have long been accused of never trying to do things for ourselves. We have consistently tried and we have consistently been denied. We have been slaughtered lambs. The state subsidized the White Sox and Sears, but when it came to my turn, I stepped up to bat and they changed the law."

State Senator William "Bill" Shaw, one of Mayor Brodie's allies, told the *Chicago Tribune*,

> "I support it [the incinerator] because the people of Robbins support it. She's [Mayor Brodie] taken lots of hits on this, a lot of heat. Here's a woman who's working on behalf of the people of her community, trying to bring economic development in, and the powers that be are saying, 'Your ten years of work don't matter,' and they snatched the rug out from under her. With the work and the hours this lady has put in, people should be rallying around her."

At this point in the project, the construction of the Robbins incinerator was seventy-five percent complete. The Robbins incinerator—one of the largest of the 30 proposed in the State of Illinois, was approximately one year from completion.

Mayor Brodie and the village's hope for the incinerator materialized in 1988 when the Illinois General Assembly, fearing a crisis of depleting landfill space that was never resolved, opened the door for the 1,600-ton-a-day $300 million burner with the Retail Rate Law, which provided lucrative financial incentives for developers. Now the legislation passed by the General Assembly threatened to turn the clock back and take away the financial incentives that attracted developers in the first place, and it threatened to deliver a massive blow to the financial growth of the Village of Robbins, a town that had struggled for economic opportunities for decades.

The Retail Rate Law would allow the incinerator to sell its electricity to Commonwealth Edison at the retail rate. The utility would in turn receive a tax rebate. Illinois was the only state to offer this subsidy to incinerator operators. It was the main reason that incinerator operators chose to locate their plants in Illinois. In March of 1996, Illinois Governor Jim Edgar signed a bill abolishing the Retail Rate Law that attracted more than 20 incinerator developers to Illinois. He made no exceptions for the two incinerators that were newly constructed: the Robbins incinerator, which was just preparing to come online and begin operations, and the Chewton Glen, Inc. incinerator that burned tires in Ford Heights that had just become fully operational. This meant that Robbins would stand to lose millions of dollars annually in host community payments from its newly constructed incinerator.

Efforts by Illinois House Republicans and staunch opponents of the Robbins incinerator received a major boost when Democratic U.S. Representative William Lipinski, of the Third Congressional District in Illinois, persuaded three Democratic state lawmakers to reverse their earlier opposition to the repeal of the Illinois Retail Rate Law. Democratic State Senators Louis Viverito (D-11, Burbank), Bob Molaro (D-12, Chicago), and Representative Dan Burke (D-23, Chicago) were enlisted by U.S. Representative Lipinski to join forces with area lawmakers who were intent on repealing the Retail Rate Law. Senator Molaro was a member of Chicago's 23rd Ward Democratic Organization, where Representative Lipinski served as committeeman. "It became obvious to me that the best way to stop incinerators is to end the Retail Rate Law. So I reached out to some Democratic friends of mine in the General Assembly," Representative Lipinski said. Representative Lipinski sent letters to numerous state legislators, urging them to repeal the Retail Rate Law, and attended several town meetings with residents who opposed the planned incinerators. Representative Lipinski said he was able to persuade the three legislators to listen to their constituents. "I talked to them [Viverito, Molaro, and Burke] about how it would affect the community in a negative manner. They had not focused completely on the ramifications," Representative Lipinski said.

Two previous efforts to repeal the law by area Republican House members opposed to the construction of the Robbins incinerator had been defeated in the Illinois Legislature in July 1994. GOP sponsors of the repeal were determined to bring the matter up for another vote in the legislature's spring session. "We welcome support from any quarter," said Republican State Senator Patrick O'Malley of Palos Park, Illinois, 18th District, who also worked for repeal. U.S. Representative Lipinski's high standing in Washington was expected to provide a shield for state lawmakers Viverito, Molaro, and Burke against Illinois Democratic House minority leader Michael Madigan and Senate Democratic minority leader Emil Jones, should they attempt to apply pressure on the Democrats for crossing the aisle and changing their votes.

In a final attempt to prevent a full repeal of the Retail Rate Law, Mayor Brodie appealed to Governor Jim Edgar in an open letter to the editor of the *Chicago Tribune* stating,

"Robbins needs help. My appeal to Governor Edgar is simple: The Village of Robbins is on death row. We need clemency.

An across-the-board repeal of the Retail Rate Law, which ten years ago provided an incentive for the developers of the Robbins Recycling and trash-to-energy facility to build in Robbins, would sound the death knell for Robbins.

Our town is engaged in a fight for its life. In addition to maintaining our own services, we must find funding to meet state and federal mandates; sewer studies, removal of underground gas tanks, and compliance with disability laws…And now, without grandfathering the Retail Rate Law to keep the state's promise to us, Robbins will lose millions of dollars promised—including a college scholarship fund for Robbins students, and any chance for growth from other quarters.

Robbins will lose a most promising opportunity to stand up with dignity. By amending the Retail Rate Law to grandfather the plant in Robbins, the Illinois Legislature will give the world the opportunity to see that economic development is finally a reality—not just an empty promise—when it is applied to poor, African-American communities working to help themselves."

Joining those who openly opposed the Robbins incinerator was then-State Comptroller Roland Burris. Roland Burris became at odds with Mayor Brodie when he made clear his position that the incinerator should be shut down. Mayor Evans Miller of Markham, Illinois, a neighboring city of Robbins, also stood in opposition to Robbins hosting the incinerator. It was believed that Mayor Miller wanted to attract the incinerator to his city. Mayor Brodie believed that Congressman Jackson and his father had aligned themselves with Mayor Miller in an attempt to sway the developers to build the incinerator in the City of Markham.

According to the United States Census Bureau, in the year 2000, the median income for a household in the Village of Robbins was $24,145, and the median income for a family was $27,602. Men had a median income of $31,667 versus $22,574 for women. The per capita income for the village was $9,837. About 30 percent of families and 36 percent of the population overall were living below the poverty line, including 44 percent of those under the age of 18 and 22 percent of those ages 65 and over. The median home value was $55,300.

Mayor Brodie and her administration were not alone in their efforts to persuade environmentalists, lawmakers, and area residents that the Robbins incinerator was not only good for the economic development of this economically impoverished community, but that it was indeed environmentally safe. Although the Village of Robbins may have been limited financially in its efforts to build support for the incinerator, the incinerator developer and prospective operator seemed to have no end to the amount of money they could spend on a dynamic and well received public relations campaign that would make the Village of Robbins and Mayor Brodie shine in the spotlight, both locally and on a national level. It seemed as if the Village of Robbins and Mayor Brodie inherited images put on by a New York City Madison Avenue public relations firm and the lobbying and legal services of one of the best Wall Street law firms that money could buy. Foster-Wheeler, Inc. of Illinois and Reading Energy Company of Philadelphia, Pennsylvania, joined together in a mega-million-dollar public relations campaign to sell Robbins as not only the right place for the incinerator, but the *ideal* place for it. Mayor Brodie was cast as the victorious government leader of the village that scored big time for the community's residents by closing the deal and landing the village a $300 million business project that would place about $3 million per year in the Village of Robbins' bank accounts, enabling it to maintain and expand operations as a municipality.

Hiring new police officers and firefighters; purchasing more emergency response vehicles, new and improved infrastructures, and building new and repairing old municipal buildings, all seemed not only possible at the time, but highly probable since construction permits had finally been approved by the State of Illinois, granting the incinerator owner and developer the right to build in Robbins.

The Robbins incinerator was certainly a high stakes project that raised the image of the Village of Robbins from a once impoverished community to one that would now have the financial resources and tax revenue that would make it just as economically viable as most of its neighboring communities like Blue Island, Crestwood, and Midlothian. The old image of Robbins that depicted the community as economically poor and financially distressed, would no longer fit, thanks to Mayor Brodie's efforts.

Mayor Brodie's stock as mayor had risen because she would assist, along with the Village Board of Trustees, to oversee and manage the expending of Robbins' newly generated revenue, resulting from the operations of the incinerator and other businesses attracted to the village. The nearly completed Robbins incinerator towered over the community, raising the hope for permanent jobs in the wake of the construction jobs that were plentiful, leading up to the project's completion. The hundreds of jobs that were created from the construction of the incinerator served as a prelude to just how powerful an economic engine the incinerator would be for the community and its residents once completed and operational.

The initial campaign to attract a waste-to-energy facility to Robbins began during the administration of Mayor Marion Smith, and the efforts culminated under the leadership of Mayor Brodie, when the village was officially granted the permit to build the facility. Mayor Brodie was also credited with obtaining significantly greater host benefits for the village in consideration for serving as the host community of the waste-to-energy facility, including a commitment of college scholarships for Robbins area high school students.

As a result of her dedication to bringing economic development to Robbins and her relentless fight to bring in the incinerator project, Mayor Brodie was invited to speak before Harvard University's Graduate School of Business. Mayor Brodie won rave reviews during her visit to the Cambridge, Massachusetts campus in March of 1994. Harvard University invited Mayor Brodie to speak because Robbins was selected as one of the school's case studies for environmental business issues. Mayor Brodie's decade-long fight to bring an incinerator to Robbins captured headlines in media outlets around the world. Mayor Brodie had spent nearly ten years studying proposals, reviewing studies and tests performed by environmentalists, rallying community leaders and residents of Robbins and neighboring towns for support, testifying before governmental agencies and regulators, and lobbying legislators in Springfield while negotiating for the project.

Her success commanded the attention of Harvard professors who invited her to the university to speak on how to initiate economic development when a community seems to have given up hope. "We don't have the inside track," Mayor Brodie told Harvard University students and professors. "We don't know what's coming. We do not know what the stakes are. We don't know what carrots or tax breaks we can offer. We don't even have sewer and water lines to offer." Mayor Brodie assured students that Robbins village leaders decided that once the village established reliable sewer and water systems, adequate fire and police protection, and dependable emergency medical and ambulance services, the village could then seek many of the other amenities the community lacked.

"We said, 'Let's not kid ourselves,' "No Jewel [Grocery] is going
to come out here. No Target [retail store] is going to come here.
No car dealership is going to come here. We have to have these
other things first."

Students posed questions to Mayor Brodie, one of which was how she had convinced developers to agree to the village's demands, and whether or not those arrangements were obtained in writing. Mayor Brodie told the students that the crucial aspects of the agreement were indeed in writing and that parts of the agreement were based on trust. "When you have nothing, you have to work with people you seem compatible with. You have to trust them." Mayor Brodie stated that developers had agreed to fund a scholarship foundation named in honor of her late husband, J.E. Brodie, who was also an accomplished educator, and her late daughter, Jeraye E. Brodie, who was a scholar in her senior year of college when she passed away. The scholarship foundation was aimed at targeting deserving and disadvantaged students in the Robbins area and providing them with money to attend college.

According to Mayor Brodie, the incinerator developer had also committed to helping build a little league field for the Robbins community and to providing a minimum of 80 full-time jobs, many of which were to be filled by area residents. Additional jobs were anticipated as a result of a planned opening of a Seaway Bank branch, expected to open in the community as a result of the construction of the incinerator, in addition to a planned fourteen-acre greenhouse. Mayor Brodie's presentation to students and faculty at the Harvard Graduate School of Business drew accolades from not only students and professors at Harvard, but also from Republican Illinois Governor Jim Edgar. In a letter written to Mayor Brodie, Governor Edgar commended Mayor Brodie for leading Robbins out of 75 years of "economic deficit." Governor Edgar further asserted, "Where once there was poverty and despair, Robbins is seeing opportunity and hope. Your determination has been key to reversing nearly a century of economic hardship, and I commend you for this monumental accomplishment."

Mayor Brodie's lecture at Harvard University caught the attention of government officials across the nation. The night following her lecture at Harvard, Mayor Brodie was flown to Washington, DC to address the U.S.

Conference of Mayors on the same issue. Subsequently, Mayor Brodie was asked to serve on President Bill Clinton's Environmental Think-Tank Group, a presidential commission on the subject. "I think it was a super experience for me and a positive image for our community—that people at Harvard and the U.S. Conference of Mayors have been inspired and at least received a different side of the issue of what is called 'environmental racism,' " Mayor Brodie said. "When they heard my presentation, each came away saying, 'This is good and important for us to hear.' "

Harvard professors Forest Reinhardt and Peggy Duxbury commended Mayor Brodie in a letter saying that students and faculty alike learned from Mayor Brodie during her visit. "In the classes since, many of [our students] have made references to your remarks, using adjectives like 'inspiring' and 'unforgettable,' " the letter stated. "Similarly, our faculty colleagues learned a lot from you over lunch."

In an attempt to attract more business and support for the Robbins incinerator, Mayor Brodie appealed to many communities and their elected offiials throughout the Chicagoland area. According to the *Naperville Sun*, a newspaper serving the western Chicago suburb, Mayor Brodie and executives representing both companies that were building the Robbins incinerator, appealed to the Naperville City Council. "I've never heard of anyone going and asking for garbage, but I'm doing it. Please bring us your garbage," Mayor Brodie requested. Over a dozen municipalities in the South Chicagoland area agreed to come aboard as customers, including Country Club Hills, Illinois and Calumet City, Illinois. Reading Energy, one of two companies building the Robbins incinerator, also made its pitch to Naperville officials. At the time, the City of Naperville was being serviced under contract by Waste Management, Inc., a giant garbage disposal company that picked the city's garbage up curbside. Reading Energy Vice President Jim DiBiasi told officials that an advantage of taking garbage to the new waste-to-energy plant is that new environmental regulations would not drive up costs to municipalities.

†

14

Environmental Racism v. Economic Opportunity

"Communities like mine have long been accused of never trying to do things for ourselves. We have consistently tried, and we have consistently been denied. We have been slaughtered lambs. The state subsidized the [Chicago] White Sox and Sears, but when it came to my turn, I stepped up to bat and they changed the law."

—Dr. Irene H. Brodie

Republican House members opposed to the construction of the Robbins incinerator were defeated twice in their efforts to repeal the Retail Rate Law. GOP sponsors of the repeal were adamant about bringing the matter for a third vote in the legislature as soon as they were confident they could muster up a few more votes that would make them successful in passing the measure.

Environmentalists alleged that racism played a significant part in determining where environmental hazards like incinerators and landfills would be located. "Environmental racism" is the term often used by environmentalists when explaining why they believe that hazardous waste sites disproportionately affect African-Americans. There has been a nationwide debate over whether corporations have singled out minority communities for dumps, incinerators, and other waste facilities. In October 1994, a research team headed by a University of Chicago economist, Donald Coursey, found that more whites than blacks lived near hazardous waste sites. The study considered thirty such sites in Chicago, which was considered the most detailed study of a single city. The study's findings concluded that no evidence of "environmental racism" was found. This conclusion contradicts a widespread belief among environmental groups. Coursey's study did not consider landfills, incinerators, and other waste facilities that were still operating or under consideration, and Greenpeace, an environmental group and leading proponent of environmental racism purports that these newer waste facilities, which the study did not take into consideration, is where discrimination and racism were most apparent. While Coursey's study was one of the most detailed studies conducted in a single city, and tends to indicate that discrimination is nonexistent, other studies have contradicted his findings.

In response to complaints that minority communities suffered disproportionately from environmental hazards, former U.S. President Bill Clinton ordered the Environmental Protection Agency and other federal agencies to stop inflicting "environmental injustice." Opponents argued that even though minority communities had a disproportionate share of environmental problems, the cause was not necessarily racial discrimination. They asserted that environmental hazards were likely to be placed in any community that lacked political power or a place willing to accept risks because they created jobs or generated tax revenue. They contended that many predominantly white communities had approved the siting of risky facilities for similar economic benefits, as have predominantly black communities.

Greenpeace asserted that waste incinerators that had been proposed for five Chicago suburbs, including Robbins, Ford Heights, and Harvey, were predominantly black, while at the time two other suburbs, Chicago Heights and Summit, were predominantly white. None of these suburbs were upper income. According to some environmentalists, lower income blacks lacked the political clout needed to fight waste facilities. In addition, environmental concerns took a back seat to more pressing social problems, such as the need for jobs and economic development in impoverished communities.

As a result of her long and relentless efforts to secure the waste-to-energy facility for Robbins, Mayor Brodie unexpectedly found herself being thrust into the national spotlight. Suddenly the Village of Robbins and Mayor Brodie were at the center of a battle being waged by environmentalists and those who demanded economic opportunity for blacks and impoverished communities throughout the United States. Now operating on the national stage, Mayor Brodie refused to yield to even her staunchest opponents, determined to fight even harder to gain economic opportunity for Robbins. Mayor Brodie's efforts drew attention from leaders around the world, environmental organizations, and governments alike.

The environmental racism theory put forth by environmentalists largely asserted that corporations had singled out minority communities for dumps, incinerators, and other waste facilities.

In his State of the State address on January 10, 1996, Illinois Governor Jim Edgar said, "Most communities do not want the incinerators and it is time we stop asking our taxpayers to subsidize them." In response to the Illinois General Assembly voting to repeal the Retail Rate Law, Mayor Brodie said it was as if her village was cut loose from wealthier neighbors [surrounding towns] just when it thought it had a grip on the rope. "Injustice is very much alive and active today. Our community feels strongly that someone out there is determined to keep us in the financial straits where we are," Mayor Brodie stated.

"Union carpenters and bricklayers have gotten work. Our truckers [Robbins truck company owners] have been contracted," Brodie asserted. "Environment is not the true issue," Mayor Brodie said. "This project has met or superseded all requirements [set by the United States and Illinois Environmental Protection Agency]. But some people think poor communities can't manage industry. The Republicans are supposed to be for business, but they are for business for the few—not for the masses," Mayor Brodie insisted. "America's promises should be meted out to the minority as well as the majority. We could add to the quality of life in the South Suburbs. How can they cut us off at the pass?"

As long as the Retail Rate Law benefited those in the white establishment who were politically and financially connected, the law made perfectly good sense. However, when the Village of Robbins, an impoverished black community that has long been ostracized by many of its neighboring white communities, secured a deal that would secure its financial independence and prosperity, then the Retail Rate Law became "bad" policy. But why wasn't it considered "bad" policy when those in the white establishment were milking the State of Illinois out of taxpayers' money for years under the same policy?

As long as the residents of the Village of Robbins were traveling to nearby neighboring white communities creating wealth for them by spending millions of their hard-earned dollars with major retailers, grocers and other establishments within those communities, that was fine. However, once the Village of Robbins attempted to gain its own financial independence and economic prosperity by obtaining the waste-to-energy facility, the village drew the ire from these same white communities that it had supported, economically, for so long.

THE INHERITANCE OF A DREAM

BILLION-DOLLAR BABY

Mayor Brodie and the Village Board of Trustees formed a review board to consider creating a local Tax Increment Financing district (TIF). This tax district would be expected to raise approximately $415 million for the financing of the waste-to-energy facility. A TIF district freezes the amount of taxes payable to local governments, particularly in this case, local School Districts 218 and 130, on a specified piece of property for a predetermined number of years. High School District 218 is comprised of Dwight D. Eisenhower, Harold L. Richards, and Alan B. Shepard High Schools. Blue Island-Crestwood Elementary School District 130 would be affected along with Moraine Valley Community College of Community College District 524, which also has taxing authority in Robbins. The local taxing bodies would continue to receive the amount of real estate taxes they had collected on the unimproved property during the life of the TIF; however, any increase in property taxes due to improvements would be returned to the project to pay development costs during the course of the TIF. Once the TIF expires, the taxing bodies would receive the full amount of property taxes on the improved property. The TIF would be expected to have a twenty-year life span.

The anticipated creation of this TIF district by Robbins village officials caused a massive outcry by opponents of the incinerator and local governments, including the local school districts. The Board of Education of Community High School District 218 became one of the most vocal opponents of the Robbins incinerator and the move by Robbins officials to form a TIF district. The incinerator property was located within a mile of the district's Eisenhower High School Campus. District 218 school board Vice President James Tate, had taken several trips to Springfield to build support from legislators opposing the incinerator. Tate argued that the tax district would be "disastrous." "That is a disastrous amount of money. Particularly since the real money comes from the state subsidy of $300 million," referring to the tax break that the incinerator would receive under the Retail Rate Law. Tate contended that with the twenty-year life span of the $415 million TIF, interest rates would add another $400 million in costs to local taxpayers for a total estimated cost of $800 million.

Opponents of the incinerator asserted that once the total amount of the tax district is added to the $300 million subsidy provided by the state via the Retail Rate Law, the Robbins incinerator would be receiving about $1.1 billion in subsidies at the expense of state and local taxpayers. Local School Districts 218, 130, and Moraine Valley Community College immediately retained legal counsel and threatened to file a lawsuit against the Village of Robbins in an attempt to prevent the formation of the planned Tax Increment Financing district. Since the Village of Robbins possessed the legal authority to create the TIF district, the only option that the local school boards had to prevent, or at least delay, the formation of the TIF district was to commence with litigation. The only measure that could possibly stop a tax district, once a village board had approved it, was through a lawsuit. Otherwise, nothing would prevent the sale of bonds by and for a TIF district.

Board of Education President Steve Heckler of Blue Island-Crestwood Elementary School District 130 expressed to local media that he expected his colleagues to oppose the TIF district being planned by Robbins village officials. "We're opposed to the incinerator," citing information gathered from the review board. "From the information that I have, my inclination is to cooperate with other taxing bodies to stop the creation of the TIF," Heckler stated.

Lee Harris, a trustee for Moraine Valley Community College, followed suit and joined Blue Island-Crestwood School District 130 in opposition to the Robbins incinerator and the proposed TIF district, calling it "the largest TIF district in Illinois," referring to the proposed tax break. "The total cost of the incinerator will be paid through TIF bond financing, and I find it incredible that any business should expect to have one hundred percent subsidies by a government," Tate commented.

Once the Retail Rate Law was repealed, and the owner and operator of the Robbins incinerator realized they could no longer operate profitably, they decided to close the facility, thereby prompting the Village of Robbins to abandon its efforts to create a Tax Incremental Financing district.

†

15

STRANGE BEDFELLOWS

"God, grant me the Serenity to accept the things I cannot change, the Courage to change the things I can, and the Wisdom to know the difference."

"Serenity Prayer"
by Reinhold Niebuhr

A famous saying, adapted from a line in a Shakespearean play and which was quoted by Charles Dudley Warner, an American novelist, goes, "Politics can make for strange bedfellows." Oftentimes political figures have to work and get along with people and organizations that they do not see eye-to-eye with, nor have much in common with. Nevertheless, some politicians need to compromise on some issues to accomplish their goals and objectives on behalf of the people they serve.

Mayor Brodie and Cook County Board President John H. Stroger had become strong allies over the years. Mayor Brodie was one of the first elected officials in the South Suburbs to support the candidacy of John H. Stroger when he first ran for the Office of President of the Cook County Board. Mayor Brodie spoke in support of John Stroger at a political rally organized by the Stroger Campaign at Captain Hard Times Restaurant near 79th Street and Dr. Martin Luther King Drive in Chicago. Mayor Brodie gave John Stroger a much-needed boost in the South Suburbs among suburban voters. Mr. Stroger would never forget the help Mayor Brodie gave him, and vowed to return the favor someday. The president of the Cook County Board is considered the second most powerful elected official in the northern region of the state; the mayor of Chicago is considered *the* most powerful. Unlike in most other states, the governor of Illinois is considered less powerful in many respects than these two local political office holders seated in Chicago.

Perhaps this power, be it actual or perceived, is derived from the influence generated by the Chicago and Cook County Democratic Machine, which not only has a firm grip on the City of Chicago and Cook County, but extends its reach all the way to the Illinois State Capitol in Springfield.

Mayor Brodie also developed a strong and ever-growing alliance with two politicians from the City of Chicago, Robert and William Shaw. The Shaw Brothers: Robert was the Alderman of the Ninth Ward of the City of Chicago, while his twin brother, William, often referred to as "Bill," served as a member of the Illinois House of Representatives. Bill would later go on to become the Mayor of Dolton, Illinois, a neighboring city, just minutes away from Robbins.

Some political insiders believed the Shaw Brothers played an important part in helping Mayor Brodie craft her political playbook. Some also believed that the Shaw Brothers taught Mayor Brodie how to best fight politically, and how to become most effective in wooing and maintaining the support of resident voters, particularly senior citizens. It is clear that the relationship between Mayor Brodie and the Shaw Brothers certainly strengthened when the Shaw Brothers joined her in combatting the opposition of Reverend Jesse L. Jackson and his son, Congressman Jesse Jackson, Jr. in their public opposition to Robbins securing the waste-to-energy project. Mayor Brodie seldom expressed her dislike of others, but to those who were in her inner circle, she minced no words about it, she did not trust either one of the Jacksons, Jesse Sr. or Jesse Jr. Mayor Brodie believed the Jacksons were both nothing more than self-serving opportunists.

Mayor Brodie attended Operation PUSH Headquarters at 50th Street and Drexel Boulevard in Chicago on several occasions to reach out for help from Reverend Jackson concerning matters relating to the Village of Robbins, and each time Reverend Jackson offered no help to the village and its residents. She believed that Reverend Jackson catered more to his Chicago base and was simply uninterested in the concerns of her small, struggling suburban village and its people, unless of course, there was something in it for him to gain.

As far as Mayor Brodie was concerned, the apple did not fall far from the tree. Reverend Jackson's son, former Congressman Jesse Jackson, Jr. who at the time represented the Village of Robbins in the U.S House of Representatives, also showed little interest regarding the concerns of the residents of Robbins. Mayor Brodie believed he pandered to the interests of his white constituents in the communities surrounding Robbins. Once the Jacksons joined in opposition against Mayor Brodie and the Village of Robbins' efforts to secure the waste-to energy project; that was the last straw. Mayor Brodie became completely disenchanted with the Jacksons.

The Reverend Jesse L. Jackson, along with his son Congressman Jackson, came to Robbins, Illinois in opposition to Mayor Brodie and the village's efforts to obtain the approval for the construction of the Robbins waste-to-energy facility. Mayor Brodie believed that their motives were driven largely by their own political and personal agendas, and not by what was best for the residents and the community of Robbins. Some village officials believed that Congressman Jackson opposed the construction and location of the incinerator in Robbins in a direct attempt to appease white constituents who were strictly opposed to the incinerator being located in Robbins out of resentment for this majority African-American town receiving the enormous economic boost that their communities were unable to benefit from financially.

It was well known publicly that the Shaw Brothers and the Jacksons were political arch rivals. The Jacksons' political machine was widely known to oppose both Shaw Brothers in their efforts to maintain their respective elective government offices. Congressman Jackson had also become widely known for his position against the Village of Robbins obtaining the waste-to-energy facility. The Shaw Brothers became known for their shenanigans involving some of their political opponents, perhaps most notably the time when William "Bill" Shaw was accused of having a man who possessed the same name as the congressman, Jesse Jackson, to run against Congressman Jesse Jackson, Jr. for his Second Congressional District seat. Some political foes, including Congressman Jackson, accused the Shaw Brothers of attempting to confuse voters in the Second District in Illinois, which could have caused Congressman Jackson to lose votes intended for him. Congressman Jackson sued in federal court in an attempt to have the other Jesse Jackson's name removed from the ballot. His efforts in court failed, but nevertheless, Congressman Jackson's bid for re-election was victorious.

There was the time when Robert Shaw, seeking re-election to the Office of Alderman of the Ninth Ward of the City of Chicago, was accused of attempting to confuse voters who opposed his re-election by fielding several of his supporters to run against him in an attempt to split the anti-Shaw votes. When a serious opponent, Walter Stallings, Jr., a Cook County sheriff's deputy, had risen in the polls as the leading candidate opposing Incumbent Alderman Robert Shaw, suddenly, Stallings Jr. became the victim of acts of intimidation believed to have been orchestrated by the Shaw Brothers. One early morning during the campaign, Mr. Stallings had awakened to discover that a few of the windows to his police squad car had been broken out overnight while parked in front of his home in Chicago's Rosemoor community. Alderman Shaw denied responsibility for the act, but some of his opponents claimed that Alderman Shaw and some of his campaign workers were behind the act of vandalism.

The power of incumbency proved beneficial for Alderman Shaw because even though he failed to garner at least 50% plus one of the votes cast in the primary election, forcing him into a runoff against another opponent by the name of Johnny O'Neal, a Chicago police officer, Alderman Shaw placed among the top two vote getters in the primary election. During the runoff election, controversy continued when Alderman Shaw accused Officer Johnny O'Neal of being a drug user and peddler, even accusing Officer O'Neal of making drug deals from inside a police squad car while on patrol. Officer O'Neal denied the allegations. Nonetheless, Shaw's claims spooked a considerable number of potential voters causing O'Neal's support among likely voters to plummet. Ultimately, Robert Shaw won re-election and maintained his seat in the Chicago City Council.

While different in many ways, Mayor Brodie and the Shaw Brothers shared a common thread—opposition to Congressman Jesse Jackson, Jr. and his father, the Reverend Jesse L. Jackson, Sr. While they were members of some of the same political organizations, including the Black Elected Officials of Illinois, their brand of politics was quite different. The Shaw Brothers had developed a reputation for being "brash" politicians who began their careers on the West Side of Chicago. It was not uncommon to hear some who were familiar with the brothers describe them as "old school, West Side gangsters." In contrast, Mayor Brodie was known as a political reformer and scholar, serving in the capacities of professor and dean at Moraine Valley Community College. The Shaw Brothers were two of the Chicago area's most controversial politicians. Their power was counted upon as an election force, particularly in the South and West sides of Chicago.

Over time, the Shaw Brothers witnessed their base of supporters in Chicago gradually erode to newer African-American leaders like Congressman Jesse Jackson, Jr. and a youthful group of leaders who were supported and slated by Congressman Jackson. This test of the Shaw Brothers' power oftentimes infuriated them, ultimately prompting them to expand their political base by moving further southward into the South Suburbs. The Village of Robbins fit perfectly into the political playbook of the Shaw Brothers. The Shaw Brothers and Mayor Brodie would ultimately join forces to form a pact that would lead to greater power for them all.

The Shaw Brothers both held elective offices in the South Side of Chicago before later moving into the South Suburbs. The Shaw Brothers recognized early on the population shift in the South Suburbs, which were experiencing a significant growth in the African-American population. Both brothers represented communities that were situated in the heart of Congressman Jesse Jackson's Second Congressional District in Illinois. This placed the Shaw Brothers in almost constant conflict with Congressman Jackson. Congressman Jackson had made it publicly known on many occasions that he simply did not like the Shaw Brothers' style and brand of politics.

William "Bill" Shaw was also an influential voice in Springfield, serving in both houses of the Illinois General Assembly, first as a state representative before being elected state senator, representing the Fifteenth District. He played a leading role in helping to win the necessary support among legislators to pass legislation that would keep the Robbins waste-to-energy facility a viable project, and to oppose counter legislation that would threaten its existence by a repeal of the state's Retail Rate Law. William "Bill" Shaw also served as Ninth Ward Democratic Committeeman, which meant that not only did he wield influence through political jobs awarded by the Chicago and Cook County Democratic Machine, but he also built political capital that could be used to influence legislation in the state house that would affect the South Side of Chicago and the South Suburbs that fell within his legislative district. The clout that Bill Shaw had in the state legislature was pivotal in helping Mayor Brodie ensure that Republicans and opponents of the Robbins incinerator could not muster up enough votes early on in the process to pass a repeal of the state's Retail Rate Law, which would have a devastating impact on the economic viability of the project.

William Shaw was later elected mayor of the Village of Dolton, Illinois and was widely criticized when he hired his brother to serve as the Inspector General of the village. The responsibility of Robert Shaw acting in that capacity was in large part to weed out corruption in the Village of Dolton. Critics argued that Robert Shaw would be woefully ineffective in the position since his brother, William, was the village's mayor. The Shaw Brothers were a force to be reckoned with in the city as well as the State of Illinois.

Love them or hate them, the Shaw Brothers have proven to be a force in the City of Chicago and the South Suburbs. Despite all the allegations of political shenanigans lodged at them throughout the years while in power, the Shaw Brothers were never indicted or convicted of any criminal wrongdoing. Unfortunately, the same cannot be said of their one-time political arch-rival and nemesis, former Congressman Jesse Jackson, Jr., who plead guilty in February 2013 to federal charges of stealing money from his political campaign fund, and who is now serving time in a federal penitentiary. Congressman Jackson's wife, Sandi, who served as Chicago's Seventh Ward alderman, also plead guilty in February 2013 to lesser charges involving tax fraud, and was sentenced to one year in the federal penitentiary. Sandi Jackson was granted approval by a federal judge to begin serving her sentence immediately upon her husband's release.

On November, 26, 2008, William "Bill" Shaw passed away as a result of colon cancer. He is survived by his brother, Robert, who remains active in politics.

16

BOSS LADY

"Many people often ask me 'Why do you still live in Robbins?' To them I say, I do not wish to leave my community, because it is home to me, and I have many more goals to tackle for the community. I'd rather be a force in a community than live someplace where there's lots of comfort and I'm not making any contributions. I'm convinced that I'm where I'm supposed to be."

—Dr. Irene H. Brodie

For many years, Robbins has often been portrayed in the media, local and national, as being one of the poorest towns in America. Since its inception, Robbins has often been cited among the nation's "worst list" for one reason or another; usually because of low income, high unemployment, and substandard housing. Circa 1920, an internationally acclaimed writer from Chicago, the late Carl Sandburg, penned a news article while working for the *Chicago Daily News*, describing Robbins as "a shanty-town where polluted waters swirled in open ditches." In the year 2014, nearly 100 years later, *Chicago* magazine's Bryan Smith penned an article describing Robbins in which he stated 'He would wonder how a place so close to Chicago could seem like such a backwater,' as he purported to convey the thoughts of the local sheriff in town, Tom Dart. In the words of others, Bryan Smith continued his description of Robbins as 'yet another poor south suburb beyond hope and *unworthy* of the effort to fix it.' As the old proverb by French novelist Alphonse Karr goes, "The more things change—the more they remain the same."

Trying to improve its image, as not only one of the poorest towns in the Chicago area, but the entire nation, Robbins has struggled for a very long time to grow its economic base, and to break away from the stereotypes cast upon it by some outsiders.

Not only was Dr. Brodie successful in her bid to become mayor of Robbins as the Unity Party's nominee, but her strong and unwavering alliance with Tyrone Haymore, the party's founder and nominee for village clerk—who perhaps at the time was riding a wave of popularity second to none among political insiders and voters—led the entire party's slate of candidates to victory. The Unity Party ticket proved to be the winning ticket, as all were elected to serve with Dr. Brodie, in their respective offices. Willie Carter, Richard Williams, and Palma James were all elected to serve four-year terms as village board trustees, and Tyrone Haymore was elected to a four-year term as village clerk. Veteran Trustee Willie Carter easily retained his position as village trustee, and his seniority rose in the legislative body, allowing him to be appointed Mayor pro tem of the Village of Robbins, thereby empowering him with the legal authority to act on behalf of Mayor Brodie, in her absence. Trustees Carter, Williams, and James also became staunch allies of Mayor Brodie, often joining together as a voting bloc, supporting legislation backed by the mayor.

Immediately upon being sworn in, Mayor Brodie had to not only find solutions to the dire financial condition of the village, but she also had to deliberate whether or not to seek Home Rule status for the village, thereby legally empowering the village to govern itself, independently of the State of Illinois. "Home Rule" is a legal form of governance in the State of Illinois that allows a municipality to govern itself with considerable independence from the state. Home Rule is a state constitutional provision or type of legislative action that results in the apportioning of power between state and local governments by providing local cities and towns with a measure of self-government, if such local government accepts the terms of the state legislation.

Mayor Brodie became a proponent of Home Rule for Robbins because she believed by doing so, Robbins would acquire more flexibility in tailoring solutions to solve its own problems as a municipality. In addition, it would also provide the village with a much greater degree of control and autonomy from the home state and not be so strictly controlled by state statutes.

The 1970 Illinois Constitution, Article VII, Section 6(a) reads as follows:

"...a home rule unit may exercise any power and perform any function pertaining to its government and affairs including, but not limited to, the power to regulate for the protection of the public health, safety, morals and welfare; to license; to tax; and to incur debt." These benefits were believed to surely lead to greater community satisfaction.

Home Rule would allow Robbins to exercise a broad range of taxing powers and to have less reliance on property taxes. With the full support of Mayor Brodie and members of the Village Board of Trustees, the matter was presented to the voters of Robbins as a referendum on the ballot. On Election Day, the majority of voters voted "For" Home Rule.

Robbins, Illinois has a mayor-council form of government, consisting of the mayor, village clerk, and six village board trustees, all of whom are elected at-large. The mayor of Robbins is the chief executive officer of the village and presides over all meetings of the city council. The mayor exercises general supervision over all village departments and also serves as the liquor commissioner. The Board of Trustees is the legislative body of village government, while the village clerk serves as the keeper of the corporate seal and records of the village.

Another one of Mayor Brodie's primary concerns was to assemble a highly qualified team of department heads that would bring integrity and hard work to village government. This effort would, at times, prove to be challenging due to the fact that the village was struggling financially and the monetary compensation needed to attract the most capable and qualified candidates was simply not in the budget. Due to these financial limitations, the process of building the best team would be a slow and difficult process for Mayor Brodie's Administration.

Although the position carries with it a tremendous amount of responsibility and requires that the person holding office be on emergency call twenty-four hours a day, every day of the year, the position of mayor of the Village of Robbins is technically a part-time position. Therefore, the office afforded Mayor Brodie the flexibility to not only honorably serve the people of the Village of Robbins, but to also further her work and her passion in the field of education.

She was able to maintain her position at Moraine Valley Community College. For years, Dr. Brodie worked long hours at the college, starting her day in the early morning, and then arriving at the mayor's office during the afternoon, where she routinely worked relentlessly late into the night.

The Office of Mayor of the Village of Robbins paid an annual salary of $16,000 to Mayor Brodie in the year 2012. Although her annual salary for mayor was minimal, Mayor Brodie earned a substantially higher salary from her position at Moraine Valley Community College. This enabled her to live comfortably while being a dedicated public servant. Her personal financial resources would also serve to aid the village during times of financial hardship. On multiple occasions, Mayor Brodie relied on her personal earnings and excellent credit rating to help secure financial lending for the Village of Robbins from commercial lenders that she had personally developed a pre-existing relationship with.

Mayor Brodie was determined to bring honesty and integrity back to village government. She had a very direct, hands-on approach with rooting out corruption and dishonesty. She once set up a sting to investigate and determine if a police officer was engaged in misconduct by shaking down patrons and vendors of the Robbins Flea Market. For decades, the Robbins Flea Market represented one of the most steady, reliable sources of revenue for the village. The police officer was revealed to have been demanding that patrons and vendors pay him money above and beyond the normal fees that were payable to the village, and was pocketing the additional money for himself. Mayor Brodie confronted the officer and ordered him to cease and desist with his conduct. Mayor Brodie also demanded the highest standards of accountability relating to the collection of money by the village's water department. Prior to her election as mayor, the water department had a reputation of being unaccountable for money that it had collected from residents for bill payments.

The Village of Robbins became very aggressive in its pursuit of federal and state grants, and various other types of funding, when Mayor Brodie hired village administrator Beverly Gavin. Ms. Gavin explored all options for obtaining grants that the Village of Robbins qualified for in order to help the village meet its financial obligations, and gain financial stability and independence.

For five years, from 2000 to 2005, Robbins experienced a significant rise in crime, particularly violent crimes such as homicides, rape, and home invasions. Police attributed this increase in crime to the proliferation of drugs in the community.

Mayor Brodie placed great emphasis on public safety. She instituted measures that would facilitate the modernization of both the police and fire departments. She utilized her personal assets to collateralize loans for the Village of Robbins and to purchase modern, state-of-the-art police cars, as the old vehicles were badly damaged and inefficient.

Mayor Brodie made every attempt to attend the funerals of residents of the village, whenever possible, especially those of young people. Attending the funerals of youth in the community always seemed to be the most difficult for the mayor because those services seemed to rekindle the memories she had of burying her daughter, Jeraye, at a very young age. If a scheduling conflict prevented the mayor from being in attendance, then she would usually pay a personal visit to the home of the grieving family, or she would send a representative of her administration in her stead. Oftentimes, you would know that Mayor Brodie was in attendance if you pulled up near a procession and saw her unmistakable silver-gray S-Class Mercedes Benz, with its vanity license plate inscribed with "Mayor," and a black and white police car behind it. Her police bodyguard would escort her through the crowd in attendance so that she could pay her last respects and console members of the family.

Officer David Leach was Robbins' police chaplain and typically served on the mayor's security detail at all public functions, dressed in his formal Robbins Police Department ceremonial uniform, topped off with a wide-brimmed, mounted hat, similar to those that park rangers or state troopers would don. When you saw police Chaplain David Leach dressed in his ceremonial police uniform, you knew an important event was being held and that distinguished people were in attendance, especially Mayor Brodie. During most of the twenty-four years of service that Mayor Brodie had given Robbins as village president, Officer Leach became a figure in the shadow of her presence. At the parades, festivals, and other outings, he would usually be there as the mayor's chauffeur and police bodyguard. And of course, at the city council meetings, he was the mayor's bodyguard among the police detail assigned to maintain order in the council chambers.

Considered by many residents to be one of her greatest accomplishments while in office, Mayor Brodie's Administration strictly enforced municipal codes that eventually led to the closing of the infamous Wynn Haven Trailer Home Park, also known as the "Trailer Homes." The Trailer Homes, as the mobile home park had been called by some residents, was a neighborhood unto itself, located in the north side of the village. This private trailer home park represented one of the worst areas for crime in the village. Located just south of 135th Street at Claire Boulevard, the Trailer Homes comprised a mobile home park that had approximately one hundred homes located on the premises. The mobile home park was privately owned and operated by Illinois political dynamo, Calvin Sutker. "Cal" Sutker was chairman of the Illinois Democratic Party, and resided in Skokie, Illinois, about thirty-five miles away from the Village of Robbins. He was so politically powerful that he was able to dodge penalties for municipal code violations at Wynn Haven Park for years, until Mayor Brodie took him to task, and vowed to hold him accountable for hazardous conditions at Wynn Haven. Ultimately, in order to save face politically, Cal Sutker sold his ownership interest in the mobile home park to a close friend. However, the living conditions at Wynn Haven Park did not improve, but drastically worsened.

Through very strict code enforcement, however, the Village of Robbins imposed fines against the new owner for several recurring municipal code violations, including creating hazardous conditions which threatened the health of the community. One of the main violations discovered by the Village of Robbins was massive dumping of raw sewage in open ditches on the grounds of the park, which led to unsanitary and hazardous conditions for residents of the park and the entire village. After multiple code infractions and warnings, Mayor Brodie and the village board moved to shut down the mobile home park.

Wynn Haven was also notorious for its ongoing criminal activity. Homicides, drug dealing, and prostitution were of routine occurrence in the Wynn Haven "Trailer Homes" Park. Conditions had become so dangerous in this part of town, certain Robbins police officers routinely delayed their response to dispatched calls reporting criminal conduct in the area. On several occasions, officers were ambushed when responding to complaints of criminal conduct in the trailer home park, having rocks hurled, and even bullets fired at them. Oftentimes, to prevent being the target of an ambush, the first patrolman to arrive on the scene would delay his or her response until backup arrived. There was only one way in and one way out of this trailer park community: Claire Boulevard. This added to the complexity of policing this community for law enforcement.

Eventually, to the satisfaction of community leaders and residents, the mobile homes were all removed from the premises, and the park was closed.

Mayor Brodie was also responsible for leading the village's effort to reconstruct the old water tower on Kedzie Avenue, and for building a new pump station. It was intended for the old water tower to serve as a backup source of water for the new tower, built near the old Wynn Haven Trailer Park. It was also intended for the old tower to serve as the main source of water for the waste-to-energy facility.

Among her many accomplishments, Mayor Brodie was able to include the village-wide water meter installation program. With the aid of the Cook County Development Block Grant Program (CDBG), the village was expected to complete the installation of nearly 1,500 water meters at resident homes so that residents would be assessed, for the first time, for the actual amount of water used per household, as opposed to a same flat-rate fee. This public works project would result in many residents enjoying a lower water bill that would be more reflective of their actual water usage. Since the village had an agreement to purchase its water supply from the City of Chicago, the residents of the village would absorb their fair share of the costs based solely on their actual individual household usage.

Mayor Brodie assembled a team to negotiate the village's debt. A waste management company serving Robbins was threatening to stop picking up residents' garbage, due to lack of payment by the village for an extensive period of time. Utility companies providing their services to the village were not paid as well, and they were also vowing to suspend their services to the village— telephone and electric companies headed the list. The financial condition of the village was so poor that the fire department was even forced to cut back on its supply of dog food for the firehouse's beloved canine, Ginger. Ginger was a Dalmatian that had become a longtime member of the Robbins Fire Department. Ginger guarded the firehouse and often rode on the fire trucks in response to emergency calls. It was clear that the dire financial condition gripping the government would touch every inch, every nook, and every aspect of operations in the village.

Robbins' supplier of water, the City of Chicago, had also joined in with other creditors in an attempt to turn up the heat on Robbins. Robbins had routinely been delinquent with the payment of its water bill to the City of Chicago. In the early 1980s, the City of Chicago had joined in on a class action suit and submitted a motion to compel the village to pay $181,000 on its nearly $1.5 million delinquent water bill, immediately.

Mayor Brodie simply could not allow this to happen. She and her staff immediately stepped in and negotiated payment terms with the village's creditors and gave them assurance that the village would make good on its commitments. This was a tremendous endeavor for Mayor Brodie because over the years, creditors had become very skeptical of continuing to extend services to the Village of Robbins based on payment arrangements, since the village had a prior history of reneging on them. Oftentimes, creditors found themselves digging a deeper hole that would never be filled by the village. Once Mayor Brodie assured creditors that this time, under her administration, things would be different and that Robbins would indeed pay its bills, vital creditors gave in, and continued providing their services to the village without interruption. This was a major feat for Mayor Brodie, who once acknowledged that, "An independent auditor wrote on the books that the indebtedness and cash flow we had, made it doubtful that Robbins would be in existence for many more years." With unwavering dedication and commitment, Mayor Brodie was able to repair and restore the village's credit rating to a respectable level, one that was deemed acceptable to both pre-existing and new creditors of the village.

Mayor Brodie would drive her Mercedes Benz to village hall, traveling eastbound, turning off 137th Street, and entering the parking lot located on the west side of the administration building. She would then proceed to her reserved parking space at the rear of the building, which was visible from both her office, and the village hall employee dining room. An employee lookout would oftentimes sound an alert, and all employees would rush to their workstations. The door would be opened by a maintenance crewman as the mayor's entrance was anticipated. She would be greeted and escorted to her office where her executive secretary, Lillian Crockling, awaited. The mayor would be briefed on all issues that were of an immediate or pending nature, and her coffee, if requested, was ready to pour. Executed on a daily basis, this had become a ritual at Robbins Village Hall.

In 2012, the Village of Robbins employed nearly one hundred employees placed throughout several departments, including police, fire, administration, water, and public works. The village operated on a budget of approximately $6 million a year, of which $3 million was generated from revenue, including resident water bills, municipal vehicle stickers, permit fees, and other fee-based village services and fines.

The remaining half of the operational budget, $3 million, was primarily generated by the awarding of state and federal government grants to the village. The village's cash flow proved to be a major concern and a top priority during Mayor Brodie's twenty-four year tenure. It was an ongoing struggle to generate revenue from a tax base that had significantly eroded, while at the same time, the village's expenses continued to mount. Payroll for employees providing vital emergency city services, such as police officers and firefighters, simply could not be delayed. Village government being in a state of financial crisis was the norm. Mayor Brodie's primary concern was how to bring back financial stability to Robbins, how to pay the bills! The village's infrastructure was suffering major deterioration. Major lines dispersing water from the old water station were eroding and leaking; major roadways in Robbins were riddled with potholes, some of which were larger than the size of an automobile tire itself.

Despite significant economic gains for the village during Mayor Brodie's tenure in office, the Village of Robbins had experienced a sharp decline in population over the past three decades. There were several contributing factors to this decline, including the demolition of the Wynn Haven Trailer Park, a spike in home foreclosures, and the voluntary relocation of some village residents to neighboring towns.

Also, the demolition of the hundred-unit Willet Public Housing Complex, located at 135th Street and Claire Boulevard, was advocated by Mayor Brodie as a way of improving public safety in the village and providing a better quality of life for residents who lived there. Several hundred of the residents that resided in this low-income housing complex were given vouchers to move into other communities. In the year 2000, the U.S. Census Bureau reported that the number of residents in the village was 6,535; and by the year 2010, that number had decreased to 5,327, signifying a drastic drop in the village population over the course of ten years. This major decline in population led an already small business base to rapidly dissipate. Residents moved out and businesses shuttered their doors.

Mayor Brodie counts among her many achievements for the village, the awarding of over $100,000 to the Village of Robbins by the City of Des Plaines, Illinois, resulting from revenues earned by Rivers Casino. Robbins, along with several other south suburban communities, including Dixmoor, Ford Heights, Chicago Heights, Harvey, and Markham, was awarded a share of the annual revenues generated by the casino, based upon poverty and income levels. Under the terms of the casino license, the northwest suburb was required to pay the State of Illinois $10 million annually over thirty years, and subsequently share forty percent of the remaining share of its take with ten designated suburbs, based upon their poverty levels. Robbins was among those ten suburbs designated to benefit, thanks to the lobbying efforts of Mayor Brodie and her administration.

By serving in the capacity of dean of educational development at Moraine Valley Community College, Mayor Brodie understood the importance of making Moraine Valley accessible to college bound students living in her town. She proved to be instrumental in working with the Regional Transportation Authority to include bus stops in the Village of Robbins to service students who resided in the village, and attended Moraine Valley. This measure significantly increased the access of college students who resided in Robbins to the Moraine Valley campus, which otherwise would have been limited, given a lack of public transportation connecting the nearby communities.

Mayor Brodie would demonstrate her leadership by joining and becoming a valued member of the National Black Conference of Mayors (NBCM). Her participation in this organization would enable her to have a major impact on not only the village that she was elected to serve, but also many other towns and cities across America. Mayor Brodie served as an executive board member, and assistant secretary of the NBCM. Her demonstrated leadership earned her the chairmanship of the NBCM's education and scholarship committees.

Her dedication and stellar leadership also earned her an honorable reputation in towns and cities across the United States. Mayor Brodie served as Vice President of the Illinois Municipal League, and over the years served, by appointment, on at least three of the gubernatorial transition teams of former Illinois Governor Rod Blagojevich; Municipal Government, Education, and Economic Development. Mayor Brodie was empaneled to serve on various state and federal advisory boards, including the advisory committee of the Illinois Environmental Protection Agency. She was a member of the Metropolitan Mayors Caucus, chaired by former Chicago Mayor Richard M. Daley. Mayor Brodie was a valued member of the South Suburban Mayors and Managers Association. She also served as a member of President Bill Clinton's Environmental Think-Tank Group, and was a guest lecturer at the Harvard University Graduate School of Business.

When Mayor Brodie joined the Black Elected Officials of Illinois (BEOI), this organization enabled her to better network with other prominent elected officials in the Greater Chicago Metropolitan Area. Harold Washington, the first African-American mayor of Chicago, was among the ranks of the membership of this elite group, along with Roland Burris, former Comptroller and Attorney General of the State of Illinois. Years later, amidst major controversy and scandal, former Illinois Governor Rod Blagojevich appointed Roland Burris United States senator for Illinois. Senator Burris filled the senate seat vacated by President Barack Obama.

In the year 2009, Mayor Brodie, while campaigning for re-election to a sixth term, perhaps faced her stiffest opposition for re-election during her tenure as mayor. Two of her once most trusted allies mounted their individual political campaigns to unseat her.

James E. Coffey was a student at Hayti Negro High School in Hayti, Missouri, under the watchful eye of J.E. Brodie, the school principal, and subsequently, the husband of Mayor Irene Brodie. Mr. Coffey and Mayor Brodie had an acquaintance with each other dating back to their high school days. Upon graduating from high school, Mr. Coffey enlisted in the United States Marine Corps. Upon completion of his duty as a Marine, he moved to Robbins, Illinois and became a political prodigy of Mayor Brodie's. Mayor Brodie mentored him, and by his own admission, she was the sole reason he decided to run for public office as a candidate for village trustee. Mr. Coffey was successful in his efforts, and ultimately served as a village board trustee for several terms. At one point, he was also considered Mayor Brodie's closest confidant. He had possession of the keys to her home and the code to the security alarm that guarded it. He was the executor of her estate. His son, James Coffey, Jr. was awarded a full college scholarship by the memorial fund established by Mayor Brodie, and suddenly, in a move that bewildered political insiders, former village trustee, James E. Coffey, Sr. announced that he would run against Mayor Brodie for the mayor's office. Like a snake in the grass, he turned on her. Needless to say, his access to her private residence was immediately revoked, and so were his responsibilities as the executor of her estate.

During the 2009 mayoral campaign, a letter was mailed to the Robbins Village Hall, addressed to the Mayor and the Village Board of Trustees. The letter alleged the sexual assault of a minor by James Coffey, Sr., a former village trustee, and executive director of the Robbins Community Center, a prominent institution in the community that organized and played host to numerous community functions involving children and adults. According to police, the letter was allegedly accompanied by an audio tape that seemed very incriminating. By this time, Mr. Coffey, Sr. had officially declared his candidacy for the office of mayor of the Village of Robbins. The alleged victim, a young teenage girl, and her mother submitted the letter along with the audio tape. In response to the letter, Mayor Brodie and the Village Board of Trustees' executive committee ordered police chief, Johnny Holmes, to conduct a thorough investigation of the allegations.

Chief Holmes conducted a thorough investigation of the allegations made against James Coffey, Sr., interrogating all parties involved including Mr. Coffey, the young girl who was the alleged victim, and her mother. Upon its conclusion, Chief Holmes announced that his investigation yielded a preponderance of evidence that the allegations made against James Coffey, Sr., were greatly substantiated, and had merit. Faced with these serious allegations and the storm that surrounded him and his political future, Mr. Coffey's quest for the mayor's office was now deemed dead on arrival by political insiders. Although he never withdrew from the race by officially withdrawing his name from the ballot, instead, Mr. Coffey ceased to actively campaign, allowing his support among potential voters to plummet and his campaign to eventually dissipate.

Meanwhile, despite the mountain of evidence that Chief Holmes claimed to have gathered during his investigation, Chief Holmes and the Robbins Police Department never arrested Mr. Coffey for the alleged criminal wrongdoing. Nor did the Robbins Police Department or the Cook County State's Attorney's Office ever file criminal charges against Mr. Coffey.

Some of Mayor Brodie's political opponents increased their criticism of her for contributing $100,000 to Moraine Valley Community College, where she taught as a professor and served as dean of educational development for over thirty-six years. She felt money given to Moraine Valley was money well spent. Critics accused the mayor of showboating with her money in the face of the economically deprived community that she served. They suggested many ways they believed the money could have been better utilized to benefit the residents of the Village of Robbins, including the financially struggling schools within the Robbins-Posen School District 143 ½.

Tyrone Haymore, once a village clerk and trustee, was a long-time trusted ally, confidant, and pivotal player in Mayor Brodie's initial successful mayoral campaign. Despite their past alliance, Haymore decided to break ranks with Mayor Brodie and run against her in the 2009 Mayoral Election. He asserted that Mayor Brodie had entered into a pact with him and other Unity Party bosses that required her to step down as mayor upon completion of her second term in office, allowing him and a few other party insiders to alternate their candidacies for election to the mayor's office, thereby enabling other party members to assume the office. Mayor Brodie rebuffed Trustee Haymore's allegations and denied ever having entered into a pact with him or anyone else. Mayor Brodie refused to voluntarily relinquish her office, instead leaving it up to the voters at-large to decide who they wanted to elect for mayor. Trustee Haymore was infuriated.

"You know I could have you bumped off, don't you?" was the question Trustee Haymore alleged Mayor Brodie posed to him in a private telephone conversation between the two, in an alleged attempt to intimidate him as her mayoral opponent. Trustee Haymore claimed he remained silent in response to what he perceived as an apparent threat by Incumbent Mayor Brodie. Mayor Brodie denied ever making such a threat to Trustee Haymore, labeling his allegation as "silly."

However, on the record, Mayor Brodie was known to share her cunning sense of humor with adversaries from time to time, and Trustee Haymore made himself an ideal target once he publicly denounced his long-time support of her, becoming a staunch critic and mayoral challenger. Mayor Brodie occasionally could not resist publicly chiding and humiliating her former sixth grade student turned mayoral challenger. "…Trustee Haymore, I suggest you correct all those misspellings in your [committee] reports," Mayor Brodie would say during public council meetings, from time to time. The expression on Trustee Haymore's face would leave no doubt to onlookers that the mayor's incendiary comments left him both ashamed and humiliated.

A bitter feud developed between Trustee Haymore and Mayor Brodie that lasted over a decade. Once considered her closest political ally, confidant, and even one of her political mentors by some accounts, Trustee Haymore now basked in the spotlight as one of Mayor Brodie's most outspoken critics and nemesis. Trustee Haymore cemented his opposition to Mayor Brodie over the years by repeatedly sponsoring legislation before the Village Board of Trustees, calling for mayoral term limits in an effort to outlaw Mayor Brodie from seeking re-election to a future term. This measure sponsored by Trustee Haymore repeatedly failed to garner enough support in the Village Board of Trustees, enabling Mayor Brodie to seek re-election as often as she chose.

During her career in government, Dr. Brodie ran for elective office nine times—three times for the office of village clerk, and six times for the office of mayor. She won all nine elections. For the entirety of her political career, thirty-six years, Mayor Brodie remained undefeated. Serving as mayor and as the highest ranking official in the Unity Party, Mayor Brodie was in command of her political party, thereby earning her the nickname, "Boss Lady."

Having served six consecutive terms in office, Mayor Brodie earned the distinction of being the longest serving mayor in the history of the Village of Robbins, Illinois. This historic feat matches the record set by former Chicago mayor, Richard M. Daley, who, like Mayor Brodie, served six consecutive four-year terms, making him the longest serving mayor of Chicago. Mayor Brodie also attained the distinction of being one of the longest serving female mayors in the history of the United States. Just prior to her retirement in the year 2013, Mayor Brodie was recognized as the longest serving sitting African-American female mayor in the nation.

†

Mayor Brodie (left) is joined by internationally-acclaimed Pastor, Father Michael Phleger of Saint Sabina Parish in Chicago.

Mayor Brodie (center) poses with members of her executive staff during the annual Robbins Rodeo and Back-To-School Festival. Left to right, Jamaico McGee, Sally Johnson, Beverly Gavin, Peggy Collier, and Margaret Newell.

Mayor Brodie thanks U.S. Congressman Bobby Rush for providing many years of great representation to the Robbins Community.

Mayor Brodie (center) takes in a photo op with her police bodyguard, Officer David Leach (left) and Robbins business owner Emmanuel "Manny" Williams (right)

Mayor Brodie (center) visits friends and fellow members of her church, Great Hope Missionary Baptist Church. Jeatha Johnson (left) and Clara Bell (right).

Mayor Brodie waves to onlookers along parade route as she serves as Grand Marshall of the Robbins Back-To-School Parade.

Mayor Brodie is honored by executive committee members of the National Conference of Black Mayors (NCBM) for her years of dedicated service as Assistant Secretary of the NCBM (1996).

Mayor Brodie (2nd from right) stands with members of her senior executive staff; Lillian Barker, Water Department Supervisor (left), Margaret Newell, Village Treasurer (2nd from left), and Peggy Collier, Human Resources Director (circa 2013).

Mayor Irene Brodie (left) welcomes Robbins native and nationally acclaimed actress, Nichelle Nichols, to Robbins Village Hall in honor of her achievements in television. Photo courtesy of Robbins History Museum (1993).

Robbins native Nichelle Nichols appears as Lieutenant Uhura in the nationally acclaimed *Star Trek* series (circa 1984). Pictured right is Samuel E. Nichols, the fourth Mayor of the Village of Robbins, and Nichelle's father (circa 1930). Photos courtesy of Robbins History Museum.

Mayor Brodie takes a "time out" for a photo op with her all-time favorite NBA player and Robbins' very own, Dwyane Wade of the Miami Heat (2006).

Mayor Brodie shares a special moment with close friend and prodigy, Robbins' very own Keke Palmer, nationally acclaimed actress.

Mayor Brodie (right) takes in a photo op with her successor, Mayor-Elect Tyrone Ward (2013).

Mayor Brodie (center) is flanked by her two most loyal political allies in the city council, Trustee Willie Carter (left) and Trustee Richard Williams (right) (2009).

Mayor Brodie stands at entrance-way to her Village Hall office and inspects the village's newly placed corporate seal (2013).

Mayor Brodie (left) engages in a lively discussion regarding her accomplishments and legacy as mayor, and the publishing of her memoirs with co-author and publisher, Vincent Williams (2013).

Mayor Brodie (left) stands with Napoleon Haney, Robbins' village administrator (2013).

Mayor Brodie (right) takes in a photo op with her executive secretary, Lillie Crockling (2013).

Mayor Brodie (center) takes in a photo op with employees of the village's Departments of Public Works and Water (2013).

Two of the Lady Bs attend the 52nd Inaugural Ball honoring the election of President Bill Clinton in Washington D.C. (1993). Chicago Heights Mayor Gloria **B**ryant is pictured (left) beside Robbins Mayor Irene H. **B**rodie. The third Lady B, Phoenix Mayor January J. **B**elmont (right), was not in attendance.

Mayor Brodie (center-standing) takes a moment to say hello to Dr. Maya Angelou, nationally-acclaimed poet and writer, at a conference hosted by the National Conference of Black Mayors (1996).

Robbins, Illinois, was home to the first African-American owned and operated airport in the United States. The airport also served as a flight school for African-Americans, some of whom went on to become Tuskegee Airmen. Photo courtesy of the Robbins History Museum (1933).

The first mayor (village president) of Robbins, Illinois, Thomas J. Kellar (seated left), and Robbins' police chief, Chief Covington (seated right), along with members of Robbins' newly organized police force (circa 1918).
Photo courtesy of the Robbins History Museum.

The first members of Robbins' all-volunteer fire department, and the Village's first fire engine. Left to right: Edward Starks, Frank Griffith, Clarence Orr, and William ReChord (circa 1923). Photo courtesy of the Robbins History Museum.

Robbins firefighters respond to an emergency call dispatch (circa 1923).
Photo courtesy of the Robbins History Museum.

Dr. Brodie (center) is joined by
her successor, Mayor Tyrone Ward
(fourth from left) and a host of
family and friends at the unveiling
ceremony renaming 135th Street in
honor of Dr. Brodie (2013).

Junior cadets and volunteers of the Robbins Fire Department line up to honor
Dr. Brodie during a ceremony renaming 135th Street, the Honorary Dr. Irene H.
Brodie Way (2013).

Mayor Brodie (center) stops by to thank members of the Robbins Fire Department for their continuous excellent service (2013).

The Force is with her: Mayor Brodie (front, center) takes in a photo op with sworn members and staff of the Robbins Police Department. Chief Johnny Holmes is left of Mayor Brodie (2013).

Dr. Brodie (left) is joined by members of her family during a ceremony in her honor. Joining her are Bertha Buckner, her youngest sister (2nd from left); her niece, Lori Alice Buckner (center); her eldest surviving sister, Evelyn Meachum (2nd from right); and Bertha's husband, George Buckner (2013).

Mayor Brodie visits U.S. Vice-President Joe Biden and his wife, Dr. Jill Biden, while in attendance at a White House ceremony honoring Dr. Brodie for her contributions to humanity during Black History Month. Official White House Photo by David Lienemann (2012).

Charles Evers, Civil Rights Activist and former Mayor of Fayette, Mississippi, makes his first public appearance at Kellar Middle School in Robbins, Illinois, where he taught 7th Grade, since abruptly leaving the school to return to Mississippi upon the assassination of his younger brother, Civil Rights Leader Medgar W. Evers. Joining Mr. Evers are two of his former students, Louise Baker (left) and Margaret Newell (2014).

Arizona State University (ASU) graduate, Mr. Chris McAfee, presents Mayor Brodie with a bouquet of roses in appreciation of her financial support enabling him to attend ASU. Left: Mayor Brodie congratulates Mr. McAfee on his academic achievements and thanks him for the roses.

Mayor Brodie (seated) is recognized and honored at a community event for her 36 years of public service to the Village of Robbins, and her endless efforts to assist college-bound students financially (2012).

17

REALIZING THE DREAM

"There have been many people that have moved back to Robbins since I have been mayor. I've had people come back and say, 'Since Robbins is changing and since you've been mayor, we're going to come back to Robbins and help you.' That makes me feel good."

—*Dr. Irene H. Brodie*

As challenging as it was, it gave Mayor Brodie, as well as all community residents, great satisfaction to be able to build and maintain a new library in Robbins. Despite the threat of having the only library in the community shuttered for a lack of financial funding, Mayor Brodie and community leaders were able to garner enough support from donors to keep the library open. Already plagued by a shortage of educational resources for the youth in the community, allowing the library to close was not an option. Dr. Brodie became an annual donor of the library, as did several friends and concerned residents of the village. Together they were able to infuse renewed life into the "William Leonard Public Library."

The new Metropolitan Rail (Metra) train station in Robbins, which is on Metra's Rock Island District commuter rail line, took a while to build, but it was completed successfully. The Metra station located at 139th Street and Utica Avenue was a flag stop, and has since been upgraded to include a warming station for riders. Metra also created a paved parking lot adjacent to the station that accommodates nearly one hundred cars.

The construction of a new Catholic Charities senior citizen building was accomplished under the Brodie Administration, and the new Dollar Store was under construction at 139th Street and Claire Boulevard in 2012. The Robbins waste-to-energy facility was also a major accomplishment for the village that was expected to bring in millions of dollars in tax revenue and provide a significant amount of new jobs for residents. Although the original contracts to construct and operate the facility were initially executed by former Mayor John Hamilton, they were renegotiated under the administration of Mayor Brodie, resulting in more lucrative benefits for the village and its residents. The land used to construct the Robbins waste-to-energy facility was given to the Village of Robbins as a gift by the S.B. Fuller Family.

The Fuller Triangle Citgo Gas Station located at 135th Street and Kedzie Avenue was built in Robbins across from the former S.B. Fuller Mansion and includes the gas station, a convenience store, and an automatic car wash with satellite retail establishments located inside the building. This represented new economic development in the community. This land was also given to the Village of Robbins as a gift by the S.B. Fuller Family.

During President Bill Clinton's Administration, the Village of Robbins received a grant in the amount of $500,000 from the U.S. Department of Justice that enabled it to hire more police officers and place a few new squad cars on the street while providing improved maintenance on the department's pre-existing fleet of emergency vehicles.

The Robbins Flea Market represents an economically viable institution for the village. The flea market is made up of many vendors and small, independent business owners that make their products available to the buying public in the community. The Robbins Flea Market has expanded and flourished for many years, located at the southeast corner of Claire Boulevard and 139th Street.

With the help and support of the late president of the Cook County Board, John H. Stroger, the Robbins Health Center of Cook County, located at 135th Street and Kedzie Avenue, was built.

Mayor Brodie's dear friend, Dr. William Jackson, who practiced internal medicine, also aided Mayor Brodie through research conducted on the ever-growing need for better health care in minority communities. Dr. Jackson headed an organization, the Northstar Organization, which promoted and lobbied for significant improvements in medical care for minorities.

The village also established a relationship with three residential real estate developers, Gerard Development, Inc., W&F Construction, LLC, and Millennium Estates. In addition, the village has streamlined the application process for building permits along with a more simplified inspection and code enforcement process. As a result of these successful relationships, over forty new homes have been built in the Village of Robbins, and multiple dwelling units under new construction have increased as well.

The Robbins Back-To-School Festival has become an institution of sorts in the village, and features a back-to-school parade and rodeo. The Thryl Latting Rodeo is a traveling group, named in honor of the internationally renowned African-American cowboy and Robbins native, that showcases the skills, talents, and contributions of African-American cowboys and equestrians from around the country. The festival has been an entertainment and recreational staple of Robbins for fourteen years. Mayor Brodie was one of the leading supporters and donors of the festival, parade, and rodeo, having pledged her personal financial support to the event in the amount of approximately $100,000. The Back-To-School event has become something that neighborhood youth have come to rely on. This event serves as a mechanism for the village to showcase its vitality, as small business owners and local vendors display and sell their goods and services. This event has especially aided Robbins' restaurants and social club establishments. The Back-To-School Festival has played a major part in the social and economic revitalization of Robbins, and has proven to be a major source of inspiration for the youth in the village, serving as a showcase of individual achievement and academic excellence.

During her tenure, Mayor Brodie administered, and credits among her accomplishments for Robbins, the Waterworks Program that under the new plan, would enable many residents to enjoy a much lower water bill based solely on their individual household usage. Mayor Brodie had also been instrumental in getting a former Robbins Water Works Bond, in the amount of $2.5 million, forgiven due to the village's economic position and inability to pay the City of Chicago for years of past due bills resulting from the village's water consumption.

In 2003, Mayor Brodie's Administration received nearly $5 million from the CCDBG, enabling Robbins to execute a major public works project, and the reconstruction of 137th Street. This major passageway leading through the village had deteriorated so badly that it had become hazardous to travel on. It also reflected very poorly on the village's ability to keep its streets in good, drivable condition. In 2004, the reconstructed 137th Street proved to be an honor for the village because it earned Robbins both local and regional awards from the American Public Works Association. Mayor Brodie had once again proven to her critics that she could get major public works projects completed on behalf of the village.

Mayor Brodie enlisted the help of United States Senator Carol Mosely-

Braun, who led the way with Congressman Jesse Jackson, Jr. in Washington, D.C. to seek forgiveness of a $2.5 million bond that Robbins had defaulted on with the United States Department of Housing and Urban Development (HUD), one of the village's creditors. The initial debt of $1.4 million was incurred in 1953 by water and sewer bonds. The village refinanced the debt in 1970, but was unable to keep up with the payments, and the debt soared by accumulating an additional one million dollars in interest. Robbins faced adverse odds because the Department of Housing and Urban Development could not wipe out debt; only Congress was empowered to erase debt.

Robbins struggled with this debt for a forty-five year period until Congress finally agreed to forgive it—something it rarely does. The debt had prevented Robbins from taking out loans to pay for improvements and prevented the village from qualifying for grants. Robbins was in dire straits financially and was not able to pay this debt. In 1989, when Dr. Brodie was first elected mayor, she began a campaign to erase the debt. She initially appealed to Washington, but got nowhere with then-Congressman Mel Reynolds or HUD. Mayor Brodie finally made headway when she got the attention of Carol Moseley-Braun during the senator's first campaign. Mayor Brodie served as one of two South Suburban coordinators for the Moseley-Braun campaign for U.S. senator. Senator Braun approached the conference committee dealing with the HUD appropriations bill and got the Robbins write-off included in the package. Tucked inside a $90.1 billion federal spending bill was a lone provision forgiving $2.5 million the village owed on the loan it took out in 1953. The bill was passed by both houses of Congress and signed into law by President Bill Clinton.

On receiving news of Congress' passage of the bill to wipe out the village's debt, Mayor Brodie responded, "I feel like I'm born again. An albatross has been lifted from around our necks. Now we can start floating bonds to do large jobs needed here."

Mayor Brodie's uncompromising commitment to improving the lives of senior citizens earned her highest approval rating. She led efforts to construct two new senior citizen residential buildings in Robbins: the Robbins Assisted Living Facility and the St. Peter Claver Court. In addition, at Mayor Brodie's urging, a third existing senior citizen building, the Edward Brown Senior Building was able to secure over $1 million for renovations. These major developments for senior citizen housing have significantly improved the quality and affordability of housing for seniors in the community. Mayor Brodie adopted the senior citizen community, in many ways as an extension of her own family. Her popularity among seniors can also be attributed to community programs aimed at providing recreational opportunities for seniors, including the mayor's year-end Christmas Holiday Party. This major community event had been a staple of the village for over sixteen years, and Mayor Brodie's unrelenting support of this event, like the Robbins Back-To-School Festival, led her to personally underwrite a significant portion of the costs of the event. Mayor Brodie was believed to have personally contributed more than $50,000 over the last ten years to make this much anticipated annual event for senior citizens possible. It is this high level of commitment and attention directed at senior citizens in the village that caused Mayor Brodie's popularity among voters to surge year after year. Her popularity among senior citizens is often cited as one of the main reasons she proved to be unbeatable as a candidate for mayor, winning six consecutive terms. With the dedicated, loyal, and unwavering support of Robbins' senior citizens standing beside her, Mayor Irene H. Brodie was unstoppable.

Mayor Brodie counts among her many achievements for the village the Community Beautification Program, which aggressively identified abandoned and hazardous properties in the village, and put them on the fast track for demolition. Mayor Brodie also ordered her department heads to be vigilant and crack down on illegal dumping in the village. As a consequence, the village instituted an anti-dumping program that awarded village residents up to $250 per occurrence when they reported illegal dumping to police, resulting in an arrest or a citation. This program proved to be very successful in significantly reducing illegal dumping in the Village of Robbins. Robbins police also stepped up their towing of abandoned and junked cars left on city streets, and in many cases, in vacant lots scattered throughout the village.

Mayor Brodie and the Village Board of Trustees successfully negotiated a host-benefit agreement that would bring additional revenue to Robbins. Robbins Community Power (RCP), a state-of-the-art waste-to-energy recycling facility, was being redeveloped in place of the once dormant Robbins incinerator facility. The new facility would serve as a wood burning power plant, and was expected to generate thirty jobs, and had committed to establishing an $80,000 per year scholarship program. The plant would have the capability of producing fifty megawatts of electricity and steam power per hour.

Over the years, Mayor Brodie and her administration had been proactive in working with multiple private organizations and governmental agencies, including the Army Corps of Engineers, to improve Robbins' infrastructure in order to prevent, or at least significantly minimize, flooding in the village. Geographically, a considerable part of the Village of Robbins is situated within a flood plain, and flooding has always been a severe problem for the village since its inception nearly one hundred years ago. The Brodie Administration had no illusions concerning what it would take to rectify the problems that resulted from recurring flooding, like extensive property damage, which would mandate that major public works projects were initiated in order to create and improve the drainage and sewer system. This magnitude of an infrastructure improvement was going to be very expensive for Robbins, especially considering the village's financial position.

Led by Mayor Brodie, the Village of Robbins sought assistance from the Illinois Environmental Protection Agency (IEPA). The village and area legislators, including Illinois House Representative Robert Rita of neighboring Blue Island, Illinois submitted a project proposal to the IEPA's Supplemental Environmental Project Idea Bank that was created as a result of an environmental enforcement case settlement. In March 2006, IEPA Director Doug Scott announced that the IEPA had been awarded $200,000 to demolish and remove vacant and burned-out structures that posed health and safety problems for village residents. This gave Robbins the necessary funding to move forward in its efforts to improve the community's environment. Mayor Brodie was grateful and thankful for the assistance of Representative Rita, Director Doug Scott, and the IEPA for aiding Robbins in dealing with its serious environmental issues. The village had identified approximately twenty-five dilapidated, vacant, and burned-out structures as the initial target for the funding initiative. These structures posed health and safety hazards when used as play areas by children and teenagers in the community. The buildings had also been used as gathering places for drug users and as storage areas for illegal drugs. The buildings clearly impeded the village's economic development activities. Mayor Brodie expanded her efforts by joining in with other South Suburban officials and IEPA Director Scott in identifying "Brownfields," which are sites where abandoned commercial and industrial properties had been targeted for cleanup and redevelopment.

Mayor Brodie made major strides in increasing the efficiency and overall performance of the police and fire departments by modernizing their vehicles and communications technology. New police squad cars were purchased and older vehicles received improved maintenance. The fire department was able to acquire new fire engines and the village's Department of Public Works received widely needed assistance with expanding its fleet of vehicles and equipment. The department was awarded funding to purchase a street sweeper, a dump truck, a snow plow equipped with a salt spreader, a new backhoe, and a tractor. Much of this was made possible by the Brodie Administration's efforts to aggressively pursue grants and low-interest loans that the village qualified for. This grant money enabled the village to modernize its emergency dispatch equipment, and to purchase other essential tools and equipment. The village was able to secure a technology grant in the amount of $257,000 from the State of Illinois that enabled the village to install cameras in and around prisoner lockup and holding areas. It also provided for the modernization of the department's records management system, which enabled police to generate official police reports with greater accuracy. The grant also made possible the purchase and installation of an audio log system that recorded all incoming and outgoing calls to and from the police department.

After many years of effort to fill the facility left vacant by the Robbins incinerator, the Village of Robbins finally reached a deal with an energy company. Robbins Community Power (RCP), a state-of-the-art energy center, transformed what had been a waste-to-energy plant into a green fuel energy center. Now, clean wood chips, such as those derived from trimmed trees and construction projects would be used to create energy, reducing the impact on landfills and limiting greenhouse gases. The Village of Robbins had, at one point, owned a fifty percent interest in the property that housed the incinerator, however, as a result of years of hardship and financial struggle since the incinerator shut down, the Village of Robbins sold its interest in the plant facility to a major creditor. The village had taken out an estimated $5 million loan from the Allied Waste Co. in order to maintain village operations. Subsequently, however, the village defaulted on the loan and as a consequence, was forced to relinquish its fifty percent stake in the incinerator property in addition to various other parcels of land and property owned by the village in order to settle its debt. In spite of this, the Village of Robbins would still benefit greatly from the conversion of the incinerator facility by RCP, as the facility is anticipated to create millions of dollars in tax revenue for Robbins. In addition, RCP committed to funding a scholarship program to help Robbins' youth attend college, and create a steady stream of revenue for local community schools.

Mayor Brodie and the Village of Robbins increased the safety and well-being of residents by creating various programs. Mayor Brodie and the Robbins Fire Department periodically hosted fire prevention and safety days, where the mayor and fire department would give away free smoke and carbon monoxide detectors to residents, particularly senior citizens. The Village of Robbins also implemented and conducted wellness checks on residents, targeting senior citizens who lived alone, particularly during days of inclement weather.

Mayor Brodie and the Village of Robbins Public Works Department would join with local veterinarians in order to provide free or discounted vaccinations for residents' pets. This program was extraordinarily successful over the years because it made affordable pet care available to pet owners in the community and resulted in healthier pets and a safer community. The village's efforts were further aided by improved communications with residents via community announcements, community news, and public affairs that were posted and broadcast on Robbins Cable TV Channels 6 and 15, Wide Open West and Comcast, respectively. This greatly enhanced flow of communication between residents, Mayor Brodie, and the village administration, resulted in significant improvements in the rendering of village services to community residents.

Mayor Brodie, by the power vested in her office, served as the liquor commissioner of the Village of Robbins as well. She was widely credited for holding the line on the issuance of new liquor licenses in the village. It had been a strategy of Mayor Brodie, village administrators, and members of the Village Board of Trustees to move Robbins in the direction of becoming a "dry" community where only a very small number of business establishments would be able to legally sell alcohol. Over the years, Mayor Brodie successfully reduced the number of liquor stores in the village by reducing the overall available licenses for issuance through attrition. Mayor Brodie seldom issued a new establishment a liquor license to sell alcoholic beverages in Robbins, and adopted a practice of only renewing the existing licenses of establishments that maintained their qualifying status with no serious infractions or municipal code violations.

In one of the final acts of her administration, just before her official retirement from the office of mayor, Mayor Brodie and the Village Board of Trustees called a special council meeting for the primary purpose of officiating a major deal with ALM Resources, LLC, the lead prospective developer of a limestone mine and quarry. Over recent years, a series of underground tests performed by chemists and engineers have confirmed that the Village of Robbins is almost entirely situated atop a bedrock of limestone, and the richest and highest quality of limestone. It is estimated that given the present-day demand for such precious stone by the construction industry, as well as the United States Government, the projected value of the limestone mine exceeds $1 billion dollars. The magnitude of this discovery is phenomenal, and professional expectations are that the limestone mine will have a greater value and yield much more economic benefit for the Village of Robbins and its residents than was expected from the now-defunct Robbins waste-to-energy facility that shuttered its doors years ago, leaving the village nearly empty handed. Not since the days during the construction of the old Robbins incinerator had such a high level of hope for economic independence and prosperity existed.

On May 7, 2013, at a special council meeting that was convened by Mayor Brodie and the Village Board of Trustees, they made it official. The Village Board of Trustees passed, and Mayor Brodie signed, a proposal creating an ordinance that authorized the Village of Robbins to acquire certain parcels of real property by way of eminent domain, and appointed special counsel in connection therewith. This action empowered the village to immediately begin the process of legally acquiring property from private owners so that the limestone development and excavation companies can proceed with excavating and producing the rich deposits of limestone. The area that will first be impacted by the excavating will be the northern-most section of the village, near 135th Street and Claire Boulevard. The mining company has agreed to compensate private property owners with enough money to obtain an equal or better home or building for operating their businesses.

Mayor Brodie and the Village Board of Trustees also officially entered into an agreement with the lead mining exploration company, ALM Resources, LLC, by approving an acquisition and development agreement between both parties. The village board also approved a resolution amendment to rename 135th Street as Dr. Irene H. Brodie Way, in honor of her thirty-six consecutive years of service to the people of the Village of Robbins." Mayor Brodie's twenty-four years of service as Robbins' mayor makes her one of the longest serving female mayors of a U.S. municipality in the history of the United States of America. Upon her retirement, Mayor Brodie was recognized as the longest serving sitting African-American female mayor in the country.

Mayor Brodie and the Village Board of Trustees approved an engagement letter that included a conflict waiver and direct payment terms between ALM, the Village of Robbins, and Deutsch, Levy & Engel, the law firm authorized to handle land acquisition matters related to the proposed industrial mining project. This agreement between the Village of Robbins and the limestone mine developers is expected to generate the Village of Robbins over $3 million a year in revenue for the next forty years, which is the estimated life expectancy for production of the limestone mining project.

One week later, on May 14, 2013 at 7:00 p.m., Mayor Brodie and the Robbins Village Board of Trustees officially convened what would be Mayor Brodie's last official regular city council meeting prior to her retirement. The purpose of the meeting was to approve the minutes of the previously held special city council meeting, held just one week prior. This action made the agreement entered into between the Village of Robbins and the limestone mine developer official and legally binding.

Upon approval of the minutes, announcements acknowledging the retirement of Mayor Brodie and other outgoing elected officials were made, and the newly elected Mayor Tyrone Ward and other incoming elected officials were thereby sworn in. The Village of Robbins had again, as it had done since 1917, successfully transferred power into the hands of new political leadership. Thanks, in large part, to Mayor Brodie and the leadership in the city council, now again, just as in 1917, when the village was first incorporated as a municipality, the Village of Robbins has a projected forecast for its residents, many bright and sunny days for years to come. It is now up to village residents to monitor conditions to make certain that the dreams, hopes, and promises are realized.

18

OVERCOMING THE ODDS

"Believe me, the reward is not so great without the struggle."

—Wilma Rudolph
Olympic Gold Medalist, Track and Field

Since its inception, the Village of Robbins has long been the subject of ridicule and oftentimes derogatory remarks, particularly, from those living outside the community. The village has frequently been stigmatized as "the poorest town in the nation," and the residents of the village have had to endure the most demeaning of negative stereotypes cast upon them for many years. Some from outside of this community have attempted to label residents of the village as poor, violent, uneducated, and underachievers. Others have tried to paint the village as a place to avoid and run away from, instead of a place to embrace and move into. However, despite such harsh branding and stereotyping of this community and its residents, there seems to be almost an infinite number of examples of quite the opposite. Positive success stories coming out of Robbins have no limit. In fact, some of the most successful people in the United States have hailed from Robbins, Illinois. This is clear proof that hard work and determination can pay off no matter where one lives and regardless of one's present station in life.

What can make a community prouder than recognizing members of its own for achieving high levels of accomplishment and, while in many cases trailblazing and breaking new barriers by opening doors that were previously closed? Robbins has an extensive list of residents, past and present, worthy of recognition. Mayor Irene H. Brodie proudly acknowledges their achievements and salutes them all.

THE INHERITANCE OF A DREAM

Through the years, many prominent and nationally recognized figures have called Robbins their birthplace or home. Although the list is endless, some of these include: Dwayne T. Wade, a professional basketball player, who plays the position of point guard for the NBA's Miami Heat; Laurence Tero a.k.a. "Mr. T," who starred as "Barracus" in the TV series *The A-Team;* Grace Nichelle Nichols, who starred as "Lieutenant Uhura" on the TV series *Star Trek*; Brian Thomas, a former Yale University student who had roles in film, television, and theatre on Broadway, including *A Different World, 227,* and *Ryan's Hope*; William Harper, a long-time resident of Robbins and actor, who has to his credit appearances in over fifty movies including *Home Alone II, The Fugitive,* and *Blankman.* Harper was also a master drummer and science engineer. He made a substantial contribution to the development of the atomic bomb in the early 1940s. Chris Hinton, an NFL football star from Robbins, played for the Indianapolis Colts from 1983 through 1989. Joe Montgomery is also among NFL players who call Robbins their birthplace and home. Montgomery played as a running back for the New York Giants in 1999. Antwaan Randle El, Jr. played for the NFL as a wide receiver for the Washington Redskins and is also one of Robbins' own.

Robbins is the birthplace of Willie May, an Olympic Silver Medalist. May competed in track and field in the 1960 Olympic Games held in Rome, Italy.

Robbins is also proud of Alan Moody, the five-time welterweight Golden Gloves Champion from 1948-1950, who won over 60 amateur fights before turning professional in 1952, when he won six straight victories. Over the duration of his illustrious career, Moody fought thirty-six professional bouts, thirty-four of which were victories and twelve TKOs.

Lauren Keyana "Keke" Palmer, a nationally recognized actress and recording artist, made her acting debut in the 2004 film *Barbershop 2: Back in Business,* and has had roles in movies like *Akeelah and the Bee, Madea's Family Reunion* and *Crazy, Sexy, Cool: The TLC Story,* she was also raised in Robbins, Illinois. Palmer has also had numerous television roles including Nickelodeon sitcom *True Jackson, VP.* Palmer earned $20,000 per episode of *True Jackson, VP,* which made her the fourth highest-paid child star on television. In July 2014, Palmer debuted as host of her own television talk show *"Just Keke"* which airs on the BET Network. This feat makes Palmer the youngest talk show host ever. Congratulations to one of Robbins' own!

Thyrl Latting is a native of Robbins, Illinois and one of America's best known and loved cowboys, who is now internationally acclaimed for his spectacular "Cowboys and Girls Rodeo Shows." Mr. Latting has brought his show to Robbins on occasion in an effort to give back to the community and inspire the area's youth.

Norman Parish, former deputy metro editor of the *Chicago Sun-Times* newspaper is originally from Robbins, Illinois, and attended Turner Elementary School. Parish, who has won several awards for his stellar performance as a journalist, started his career as a reporter covering the Village of Robbins, neighboring South Suburbs, and Chicago's Southside for *Citizen* newspaper. Parish is a former board member of the National Association of Black Journalists.

The Village of Robbins holds a very special place in the field of education, not only in the Chicago metropolitan area, but nationally. Mr. and Mrs. J.E. Brodie recruited a countless number of African-American educators, in many cases providing them with their first opportunity to teach. J.E. Brodie recruited African-Americans from around the country to teach at Kellar Middle School and Blue Island High School, both schools where he served as principal. Robbins was a major training ground of sorts for African-Americans in the fields of education and school administration. They were openly embraced and trained as educators in Posen-Robbins School District 143 ½, while African-Americans were still being widely discriminated against in the Chicago Public School System. J.E and Irene Brodie's impact on helping African-Americans obtain and develop careers in education is immeasurable. It is certainly befitting and an honor that Bernice Childs Elementary School and Kellar Middle School, both being located adjacent to the other and within School District 143 ½, have been recognized for excellence in academic performance and their students' overall test scores, ranking them among the best schools in the nation, comparatively.

Robbins has produced an almost endless list of trailblazers in the field of medicine, some of whom are heading public health departments in cities throughout the nation. One such medical trailblazer is Dr. Woody M. Winston, M.D., a Doctor of Internal Medicine. Dr. Winston was the first African-American to open a medical practice in the Village of Robbins.

Twin brothers Drs. Marvin and Merrill Chandler both built great reputations for themselves by becoming Doctors of Pharmacy. After succeeding in positions at Walgreens, a national drugstore chain, they ventured out on their own and established Chandler's Drug Store in Robbins, Illinois. The overwhelming success of their store led the Chandler Brothers to become not only highly respected and distinguished doctors in the community, but also two of the most successful and revered entrepreneurs in town. Dr. Marvin Chandler also served as a member of the Robbins Village Board of Trustees.

Robbins' own Dr. Kenya Jamison-Martin became a very distinguished medical doctor and subsequently, she joined the United States Air Force and earned her wings as a pilot. Dr. Jamison-Martin's academic and professional success earned her an appointment to the White House medical staff during the administration of President George W. Bush. Dr. Jamison-Martin received training on how to fly and operate Air Force One, and she is believed to have served as a back-up pilot aboard Air Force One, the official aircraft that carries the President of the United States.

In a non-conclusive attempt to list other great doctors from Robbins, Illinois, we will mention Dr. Home L. Allen, a Doctor of Dentistry, Dr. Lynn R. Walker, a Doctor of Internal Medicine, Dr. Ansel T. Johnson, Doctor of Optometry, Dr. Fred Gletten, a Doctor of Gastrointestinal Disorders, Dr. Michael Thomas, a Doctor of Gynecology and Obstetrics, Dr. Dennis Riston, a doctor specializing in public health, Dr. Forrest Jones, a Doctor of Internal Medicine, Dr. Glen Trammell, a Doctor of Internal Medicine, Dr. Stanley T. Harper, a doctor specializing in public health, Dr. Allen T. Jackson, a doctor specializing in public health, and Dr. Terrod B. Butler, a Doctor of Pediatrics.

And last but not least, the Village of Robbins has made a monumental contribution to American aviation as an incubator of sorts for the Tuskegee Airmen. Robbins was the home of the first flight school and airport in the nation that was built, owned, and operated by African-Americans, and the airport welcomed black pilots with open arms when many white-owned and operated airports across the nation, including Chicago's, forbid them from flying their planes in and out.

As an old saying goes, "One thing for certain, two things for sure," hard work pays off, no matter where you live or what your current station in life might be!

19

PAYING IT FORWARD

"I've learned that you shouldn't go through life with a catcher's mitt on both hands; you need to be able to throw something back."

—*Dr. Maya Angelou*

❧

Dr. Irene H. Brodie established the J.E. Brodie and Jeraye E. Brodie Memorial Scholarship Fund to help deserving and qualified high school students residing in the Village of Robbins pursue their dream of attending college. The Brodie Memorial Scholarship Fund has helped hundreds of academically gifted and deserving high school students attend colleges across the nation, including Florida A&M University, University of Illinois at Champaign, University of Illinois at Chicago, Chicago State University, Moraine Valley Community College, Eastern Illinois University, Saint Xavier University, Northern Illinois University, and many other colleges and universities. The Robbins Council for Educational Opportunity was established to assist with administering the scholarship funding to qualified, deserving students. Mayor Brodie received financial commitments from corporate sponsors to fund her efforts in providing scholarships for Robbins students. Foster-Wheeler Illinois, Inc. and Reading Energy Co. became donors to the J.E. and Jeraye E. Brodie Memorial Scholarship Fund as well, pledging over $100,000 a year.

The Scholarship Fund had an established criterion that each student applicant was required to meet in order to qualify for financial assistance. Applicants were required to submit an essay detailing their interest in attending college and why they should be awarded a scholarship. Applicants were also expected to demonstrate successful academic performance while in high school, and candidates who were awarded scholarships were expected to achieve and maintain an acceptable and satisfactory grade point average while in attendance at their selective colleges.

Scholarships to qualified applicants were typically awarded in an amount ranging from $3,000 to $15,000 per student per academic year, depending upon the student applicant and the college or university selected, and the applicable tuition costs along with other related expenses. Each student awarded a scholarship was required to contribute to their community by devoting their time to serve 400 hours of community service over the duration of their four-year scholarship, and recipients were usually assigned community service tasks through the Robbins Village Hall.

The Robbins Council for Educational Opportunity was organized for the purpose of administering and managing the scholarship fund. Board members were selected and policies and procedures were put in place. Foster-Wheeler Illinois, Inc. and Reading Energy Company, the incinerator's operator and developer, played a significant part in the organization pursuant to the terms of their commitment to contribute over $100,000 annually to the scholarship fund. Jacoby Dickens, then-chairman of Seaway National Bank, also served as a board member.

For many years, Dr. Brodie had made it an annual tradition to personally award the valedictorian and salutatorian at Thomas J. Kellar Middle School with $2,000 in scholarships for their exceptional academic performance. Dr. Brodie also routinely awarded scholarships to needy students who, under certain circumstances, did not meet the standard criteria set by her scholarship fund. It was not uncommon for students or their parents to request financial assistance from Dr. Brodie, and to immediately receive monetary support from her without having to undergo a formal application process. Dr. Brodie went above and beyond the call of duty to help those in need.

After helping to garner financial support for several hundred disadvantaged college-bound students, fewer things brought more enjoyment to Mayor Brodie, as well as other village residents, than seeing those students return home upon successful completion of each academic school year and ultimately, graduation. It was a feeling that would make anyone bask in the light and declare with a heart-felt smile, "Mission Accomplished!" The scholarships awarded and the ongoing fundraising efforts, and personal financial contributions made by Dr. Brodie are estimated to exceed $750,000.

Dr. Brodie's assistance to young adults was not limited to academic scholarships; she helped some with housing as well. She provided some youngsters with money for housing they otherwise would not have been able to afford. In a few situations, she even accommodated young adults who were homeless by allowing them to reside temporarily at her home. Many people are not aware of these good deeds performed by Dr. Brodie. However, Dr. Margaret Lehner, one of Dr. Brodie's good friends and former colleagues at Moraine Valley Community College, recalls a time when Dr. Brodie provided a young woman who was in need of shelter with a room at her personal residence. Dr. Lehner also vividly recalls that there were times when Dr. Brodie personally escorted students who were registered to attend classes at Moraine Valley to the Bursar's Office to issue payment for the students' tuition for the academic semester. If there were personal problems or trying times that a youngster was experiencing, Dr. Brodie sincerely attempted to help when and where she could. However, there was one particular case where Dr. Brodie had agreed to offer financial assistance to a young man who had sought her help with paying his tuition for the semester; Dr. Brodie escorted the young man to the Bursar's Office with her checkbook in hand to pay the student's tuition, only to be informed by representatives of the Bursar's Office that the student's tuition was already fully covered by government-issued grants. Fortunately, the student's scheme was quickly revealed to Dr. Brodie before she needlessly expended her money. Despite rare incidents like this, Dr. Brodie never wavered away from her sincere commitment to help those youngsters who were in need of financial help to attend college.

On February 4, 1995, Dr. Brodie was recognized and praised for her outstanding support and commitment to the cause of black higher education by the National Pre-Alumni Council of the United Negro College Fund. The council presented Dr. Brodie with its award of appreciation for her continued efforts.

Irene Hale Brodie started her career as a young teacher with the mission to help educate youngsters. She continued on that mission for many years as she advanced her career in both education and government. After having served in the fields of education and government for well over half a century, never once did Dr. Brodie allow her mission of helping educate deserving and gifted students become derailed. For over sixty-five years, leading up to her official retirement from the Office of Mayor of the Village of Robbins, Dr. Irene Brodie stayed on course with her mission. She accomplished her mission by helping a countless number of others reach their individual goals. And to all those achievements, we can declare "Mission Accomplished, and a job well done!"

The following represents a partial list of colleges and universities attended by scholarship recipients of The J.E. and Jeraye E. Brodie Memorial Scholarship Fund:

Arizona State University

California State University at Sacramento

THE INHERITANCE OF A DREAM

Chicago State University

Eastern Illinois University

Florida A&M University

Governors State University

Illinois Academy of Design & Technology

Illinois State University

Illinois Wesleyan University

International Academy of Design & Technology

Lewis University—Romeoville

Moraine Valley Community College

Northern Illinois University

Rock Valley College (Illinois)

Saint Xavier University (Chicago)

South Carolina State University

Southern Illinois University

University of Illinois at Chicago

University of Illinois—Urbana/Champaign

Western Illinois University

†

20

R.P.D. BLUES

"If thou faint in the day of adversity, thy strength is small."

—Proverbs 24:10

ⸯ◠◡◠

O ne of the greatest challenges facing the mayor of any city is the matter of public safety. This would prove to be no exception for Mayor Brodie. The Robbins Police Department presented multiple problems that commanded her attention. The Village of Robbins police department had long been the subject of criticism for the handling of some of its criminal cases. In January 2013, as a result of an investigation conducted by Cook County Sheriff Tom Dart, the department had received widely publicized criticism for its handling of cases involving rape victims. It was discovered and reported that approximately 200 rape kits had languished untested in the police department's evidence room, some for nearly thirty years. This grossly negligent conduct compromised a countless number of criminal cases and investigations. According to Sheriff Dart, the majority of the police department's officers were poorly trained, and their reports lacked so much basic information that they proved useless to prosecutors. As had been the case in years past, the Cook County Sheriff's Department stepped in to assist the Robbins Police Department wherever possible and to also investigate the department's conduct.

Back in 1991, Mayor Brodie fired then-police chief, Johnny Holmes. Shortly thereafter, she re-hired Holmes after two of her strongest allies on the Village Board of Trustees, Trustee Willie Carter and Trustee Richard Williams, persuaded her to reconsider and reinstate Johnny Holmes. Chief Holmes had come under fire at the time because he had publicly announced his support of one of Mayor Brodie's political arch rivals in the city council, Trustee Gregory Wright, against Mayor Brodie's re-election efforts. Trustee Wright also served as superintendent of public schools for Posen-Robbins School District 143 ½, and was one of Mayor Brodie's most vocal critics in the Robbins city council. Chief Holmes also served as a board member of High School District 218, which oversaw the operations of area high schools in Blue Island and other neighboring communities surrounding Robbins.

Chief Johnny Holmes had served as the chief of police for the Village of Robbins for many years. For most of the time, he was able to avoid being the focus of attention by the local news media. However, during the last year of his tenure, he repeatedly made the headlines of local news outlets. One evening, while off duty, Johnny Holmes was stopped by neighboring Midlothian police after a motorist passing by him phoned police and alleged that a man was driving recklessly and had almost struck the vehicle of at least one of the motorists that had passed by. Midlothian police pursued and detained Chief Holmes and determined that he was driving while intoxicated.

In an effort to minimize her daily intervention in police affairs, Chief Holmes devised a plan to confiscate Mayor Brodie's police radio and scanner so that she would be further removed from the daily operations of the police department. He persuaded Mayor Brodie to turn in her radio so that it could receive a "maintenance check" and undergo "necessary repairs." He never returned the radio and upon her regular inquiries as to the status of repair, Chief Holmes repeatedly communicated, "It is still being serviced." He maintained this response until the Mayor eventually stopped inquiring.

As time passed, Mayor Brodie became less involved in the direct operations of the police department, and instead focused most of her attention on matters related to the village's financial management and economic growth. During the mayor's final year in office, the general operations of the village were managed by Robbins' executive administrator, Napoleon Haney. Mr. Haney was not at all impressed by the overall on-the-job performance and track record of Chief Holmes, and the negative headlines garnered by Chief Holmes from local media, only further strained their relationship. Mayor Brodie's health issues had become more evident and she adjusted her schedule primarily to include only the more pressing issues facing the village. She continued to preside over all city council meetings, which regularly convened bi-weekly, on Tuesdays, at the village hall.

Several months after his initial arrest for driving under the influence (DUI), Chief Holmes was once again driving in neighboring Midlothian when police observed his vehicle moving improperly and sporadically between lanes. They pursued, and once again, detained him. Since Chief Holmes' previous infraction of the law had gained widespread media attention, the Midlothian police officer who stopped him this time, had familiarity with his driving record and prior arrest in Midlothian for a DUI. The police officer immediately suspected that Chief Holmes was again driving under the influence of alcohol. When informed he would have to take a sobriety test, Chief Holmes replied with astonishment, "Oh, Wow." This time, Chief Holmes was reportedly so inebriated he did not even know what town he was in.

While poking his chest with his index finger, Chief Johnny Holmes confidently exclaimed, "When Mayor Brodie leaves—I'm leaving! I don't need to be here. I can be out fishing," recalled inside sources at village hall. Village administrator, Napoleon Haney, discovered that there was a code of silence as it related to Chief Holmes, and a code word used to describe him was "untouchable." He realized that no matter how hard he tried, he would never be able to terminate the employment of Chief Holmes because he was "untouchable." Chief Holmes was the unofficial "Boss" of the Unity Party since Mayor Brodie was nearing retirement and had relinquished many of her responsibilities as head of the party. Since his rehiring, Chief Holmes firmly re-established himself as a trusted, loyal supporter of Mayor Brodie and the Unity Party agenda, thereby earning him the strong support of Mayor Brodie. It was very clear that Chief Holmes had near complete autonomy at village hall. In addition, Chief Holmes could count on two of his staunchest Unity Party allies who sat on the Village Board of Trustees to back him, if needed. Trustees Willie Carter and Richard Williams had gone to bat multiple times in the past for Chief Holmes.

Chief Johnny Holmes was arrested twice in Midlothian for driving under the influence, and the second time was the straw that broke the camel's back. Now, Village Administrator Napoleon Haney had Chief Holmes positioned with his back up against the wall, exactly where he wanted him, and he went in for the kill. News outlets in and around Chicago could not resist the opportunity to run stories about the DUI incidents which resulted in embarrassment for the Robbins Police Department and the Brodie Administration. As a result, upon the urgent request of Mr. Haney, Mayor Brodie met privately with members of the Robbins Village Board of Trustees, including Trustees Carter and Williams, and reached the decision to expedite the retirement of Chief Holmes. Retiring, not firing was the optimal choice. Mayor Brodie appointed police Captain Jerome Guinn to serve as interim police chief.

Upon Mayor Brodie's retirement and amid the police department scandal surrounding the department's neglect to properly process hundreds of rape kits,

THE INHERITANCE OF A DREAM

Mayor Tyrone Ward appointed a new police chief, Melvin Davis, only to have to fire Chief Davis about five months later amid a state investigation into the apparent falsification of the employment history of a part-time police captain. The Illinois Law Enforcement Training and Standards Board, an official state regulatory agency, sent Mayor Ward and Chief Davis a letter on November 14, 2013, threatening to pursue charges against Douglas J. Smith for impersonating a police officer and unlawful use of weapons, if he stayed on the police force. In the letter, Kevin McClain, the director of the state regulatory agency, implied that Mayor Ward and Chief Davis could also be charged with official misconduct if Officer Smith was not immediately dismissed. Officer Smith, a 61-year old resident of nearby South Holland, Illinois was hired to head the Robbins Police Department's Internal Affairs Bureau, and he carried a handgun throughout his three months of employment as a Robbins police captain, even though he failed to complete mandatory firearms training as required under Illinois state law. In addition, authorities in the City of Los Angeles, and the states of New Jersey and Georgia, where Officer Smith claimed to have worked in law enforcement, told investigators for the state training board that their records did not indicate that Smith ever worked for them.

As proof of his past employment with the Los Angeles Police Department (LAPD), the Illinois Law Enforcement Training and Standards Board alleged Officer Smith submitted to its investigators a photocopy of an LAPD badge bearing the number 714—the badge number of the fictional character Sergeant Joe Friday from the old TV show, *Dragnet*.

†

21

EXIT INTERVIEW

~୭

At 2:30 p.m. on May 01, 2013, approximately two weeks prior to the day of her official retirement, Mayor Irene Brodie agreed to an interview. This interview conducted at her private residence represents her last official interview while holding office.

Vincent Williams: Hello and thank you Mayor Brodie for welcoming me into your home, and allowing me to conduct this interview.

Mayor Irene H. Brodie: You're welcome. It's a pleasure to have you here.

VW: Soon you'll be retiring from public life after having served in various positions for several decades, how does it feel to be retiring as mayor after having served the Village of Robbins in that capacity for twenty-four years?

Mayor Brodie: It feels great. I just want to enjoy life and relax now. It has been a long time and I'm tired!

VW: I'm sure, because you served the village as its official village clerk for twelve years prior to being elected mayor, right?

Mayor Brodie: That's absolutely right. I was elected to three four-year terms by the people to serve as Robbins' village clerk.

VW: What is one of the most difficult challenges that life has presented you with?

Mayor Brodie: The day my daughter, Jeraye, died was probably the toughest day of my life. She was a beautiful girl—young woman, and she was very, very bright. Back at that time, I had almost given up, completely. I felt as if I had lost everything. It took me a long time, and it was a very trying time for me, but with the support and encouragement of family, friends, and some of my colleagues at Moraine Valley who pushed me to achieve my doctoral degree, I was able to make it through that period of my life.

THE INHERITANCE OF A DREAM

VW: I have heard that you credit your daughter, Jeraye, with being the catalyst for you initially seeking election as mayor of Robbins?

Mayor Brodie: That's absolutely right. It was Jeraye's dream to become actively involved in the community. She was really ahead of her time. She had a desire to be of public service to those who needed help early on in her life. She noticed some of the inequities and disparities affecting Robbins while she was very young. She once said to me, "Mom, when I finish my bachelor's degree, I'm going to come back and work with Robbins. Somebody's got to get out there and do it." Her intentions and deeds of goodwill certainly made me proud and have had a long, lasting impact on my desire and commitment to serve this community and its people.

VW: So, in essence, it would seem that with the passing of your daughter, Jeraye, that you were the beneficiary of her dream, and had fulfilled a mission that she had set out to embark upon, but was unable to accomplish due to her illness and untimely death?

Mayor Brodie: That's true. I can say that it was a joint mission because it was that fire and determination that she had for helping this community that elevated my motivation and determination to do something about the problems that we face as well, and filled with that spirit, I decided that I would seek the office of mayor, a position that I really believed that I could have great impact in to effect change for the better.

VW: Do you believe that you accomplished the mission that Jeraye had intended to pursue, and the objectives that you adopted?

Mayor Brodie: Oh, unquestionably, yes! Robbins is a much, much better place today than when I first became mayor some twenty-three years ago. Back at that time, many folks were questioning whether or not the village would survive because it was in such bad financial shape. It was really teetering on the brink of bankruptcy. The village's creditors had lost all confidence in the village's ability to pay its debt, and either had already interrupted or was threatening to cut off most, if not all, city services to the village and its residents.

VW: What do you think of President Obama's performance in office?

Mayor Brodie: I think he's doing a wonderful job, especially given all the unnecessary opposition that he's constantly faced with. I love him and his wife, Michelle. I think they're doing a great job. I believe that his healthcare initiative, [Obama Care] will have a great impact for poor and working-class people, finally providing access to affordable healthcare like never before. I also applaud him for sticking to his commitment to make certain that women in the workforce receive equal pay for performing the same duties as their male counterparts.

VW: I know you've previously mentioned that you've met Mr. Obama on several occasions, particularly when he served as a state senator in Springfield. What was he like to work with as a legislator then?

Mayor Brodie: He was very helpful. I remember when I first met him during a road trip that I and a few colleagues had made down to the State Capitol in Springfield. I had stopped at a convenience station to grab a bite to eat and fill the car up with gas, and it was there that Senator Obama asked me how I was doing, and if I needed any help or needed him to escort me down to the Capitol. He was just a very fine and sincere young man. I knew then that he'd have a bright future ahead of him.

VW: Speaking of the White House, you attended an event hosted at the residence of Vice President Joe Biden in honor of Black History Month. How was that?

Mayor Brodie: It was lovely! President Obama issued a proclamation acknowledging and honoring African-American women who have made a positive difference in their communities. I was honored that the president and vice president invited me to The White House to acknowledge my contributions to humanity and to be a part of that special event.

VW: Mayor Brodie, you became a donor to Moraine Valley Community College, contributing $100,000 to the college. You received a lot of criticism from some community leaders in Robbins, as well as quite a few residents. Why do you think you received so much criticism from some folks in Robbins about your donation to Moraine Valley? And what would you say to all those who say that the money could have been better utilized in your struggling community of Robbins?

Mayor Brodie: Yes, I am a proud donor of Moraine Valley Community College, and I've never been prouder! Moraine has been a monumental force for good and has played a very important role in helping disadvantaged and deserving students from not only Robbins, but the entire South Suburban Region, with gaining access to a quality education. Over the last three decades, Moraine Valley has invested in many students in Robbins by opening up a satellite branch in the community itself and developing and implementing programs to provide opportunities to a countless number of students today. I can think of no better institution to help further its goals than that of Moraine Valley, a college that I have had the benefit of serving as dean and working with as an elected official to further the much-needed education of our youth.

THE INHERITANCE OF A DREAM

It is always easier for some people to criticize than to get themselves engaged to provide real solutions to some of the problems we face. Besides, I never give too much weight to what my critics and opponents have to say, especially during an election season. None of them have had as great of an impact on improving the quality of education and the level of access to those who otherwise might not have access, than Moraine Valley. I say a contribution to Moraine is clearly an investment in opportunity for disadvantaged and minority youth who yearn for a quality and affordable college education.

VW: Thank you Mayor Brodie, for taking the time out of your busy schedule and allowing me to conduct this interview. It has been very informative, and I truly wish you the best upon your retirement from the mayor's office.

Mayor Brodie: You're quite welcome, young man, and I do hope to be able to enjoy more of my time to myself soon. It has been a very long time since I've had a real opportunity to get some rest. I'm exhausted. After all these years, I'm tired!

†

22

HONORING A GREAT LADY

"...Today, we stand on the shoulders of countless African-American women who shattered glass ceilings and advanced our common goals. In recognition of their legacy, let us honor their heroic and historic acts for years to come."

—*President Barack H. Obama*
A Proclamation by the
President of the United States of America,
National African-American History Month 2012

On May 17, 2013, several hundred supporters including friends, former students, public officials and relatives of Dr. Irene H. Brodie came from all across the nation to convene at the Tinley Park Convention Center to honor and pay tribute to her. Dr. Brodie officially retired from her position as mayor of the Village of Robbins on Tuesday, May 14, 2013, immediately upon the swearing in of her successor, Tyrone Ward, as Robbins' new mayor, entering a new era. Prior to being elected mayor, Tyrone Ward served as a trustee of the Village of Robbins. As a member of the Village Board of Trustees, Trustee Ward, oftentimes stood in opposition to Mayor Brodie, becoming somewhat of an arch critic of Mayor Brodie and her administration.

On Saturday, May 18, 2013, residents, civic leaders, and village officials gathered at 135th Street and Springfield Avenue in Robbins to dedicate the re-naming of 135th Street to "Dr. Irene H. Brodie Way." By resolution of the Village Board of Trustees, the entire stretch of 135th Street that runs through the village was officially re-named in honor of Dr. Irene H. Brodie for her 36 years of combined service to Robbins as clerk of the village, and subsequently as mayor. At the recommendation of former village clerk and trustee Tyrone Haymore, the Robbins Village Board of Trustees selected 135th Street to honor Dr. Brodie. This street is symbolic because it was there that Dr. Brodie launched her political career. She taught and served as assistant principal at Turner Elementary School located on 135th Street, and her home is located nearby as well.

The Village of Robbins commemorated Dr. Irene H. Brodie's service as mayor by designing and issuing the Robbins 2013 motor vehicle sticker in honor of Dr. Brodie's 24 years of service.

During the final months prior to her retirement from public service, Dr. Brodie enjoyed sharing more of her time with family and friends. She has now been able to devote more of her time to relaxing and traveling. She has found that completely remodeling her home has replenished and reinvigorated her. She now finds that she has more time for cooking and enjoying many of the things that are so important to her. She often invites family and friends to her home during harvest season to share in the experience of picking pears from her treasured pear tree in the backyard.

Dr. Brodie has remained greatly devoted to Great Hope Missionary Baptist Church and its Pastor Walter L. Cook. Dr. Brodie cherishes the added time that she now has to worship and support church causes and events. She gives all praises to God and cherishes her spiritual upbringing, an upbringing which pushed her to pursue a lifelong commitment to public service with a legacy of unparalleled achievements.

Dr. Brodie is an avid basketball fan. She rarely misses a Chicago Bulls game or games played by her favorite team, the Miami Heat. Of course her main attraction to the Miami Heat is one of Robbins' favorite sons, Dwayne Wade or "D-Wade!" as Dr. Brodie often shouts while watching her favorite shooting guard at work. Dwayne Wade was a first round NBA draft pick in 2003. Standing 6 ft. 4 in. tall and over 200 pounds, Mr. Wade's stature and talents are almost as big as his heart and compassion for his community, youth, and people as a whole. Dr. Brodie and the entire Wade Family have developed a close friendship over the years, and she often applauds Dwayne for his good ambassadorship for his hometown and his generous financial support over the years for the betterment of the village. Siohvaughn Funches-Wade, Dwayne's ex-wife, was one of the first to be awarded the J.E. and Jeraye E. Brodie Memorial Scholarship by Mayor Brodie, enabling her to attend Eastern Illinois and Chicago State Universities prior to becoming nationally recognized. Dr. Brodie at one point assisted Miss Funches with financial aid for temporary housing as well. Dr. Brodie is very proud to call "D-Wade" one of Robbins' very own. Her unwavering allegiance as a Miami Heat fan is only matched by her enthusiasm for the Chicago Bulls. Needless to say, Dr. Brodie's ideal matchup is when the two teams face off. Dr. Brodie often says that a Bulls versus Heat matchup, while enjoying an ice cold Dr. Pepper and some Portillo's fast food carryout, will make for some ideal recreation time for her while in retirement.

Dr. Brodie enthusiastically embraces her retirement from a life in public service because it will enable her to spend more time with her family, especially her niece and nephew, Lori Allison Buckner and Byron Keith Buckner. Both Lori and Byron are now established in their careers as educators. Following in their mother, Bertha's, and Auntie Irene's footsteps, Lori is now a teacher in the metropolitan Chicago area, and Byron works for the Kansas City Public School System. Dr. Brodie looks forward to continuing to serve as a force for excellence in her niece's and nephew's lives.

Dr. Irene H. Brodie makes it clear, in no uncertain terms, that as she retired from her life of public service, she has left the Village of Robbins in a much better position than when she was first sworn in as mayor, 24 years ago. She believes that she has left behind an enduring legacy that exhibits her high level of determination and strong will to achieve excellence in education and public service. She has set the bar high for measuring integrity, and she has kindled a spirit among residents that summons their dedication to community service and individual achievement. Dr. Brodie is confident that she has greatly contributed to building a stronger foundation for the village that will help it sustain and nurture itself for many years to come.

After great consideration, Dr. Brodie decided to contribute some of her financial and personal assets to the Robbins History Museum. She has been a financial contributor and she plans to donate all of her mayoral ball gowns. The value of several of these high quality, custom designer silk gowns is priceless. In addition, Dr. Brodie has agreed to donate other items that are directly related to her service to the Village of Robbins as its mayor. Dr. Brodie hopes that these gifts will inspire future generations of youth, and provide them with the ability to share in her spirit of giving and service to the community.

At the "Honoring a Great Lady" Gala on May 17, 2013, there were several guest speakers who highlighted the contributions made by former Mayor Irene Brodie. United States Congressman Danny K. Davis commented on how he witnessed Mayor Brodie fight for funding to help keep the Village of Robbins alive and functioning during a time when Robbins was facing grave economic conditions. Attorney James Coffey, Jr. praised Dr. Brodie for helping to make possible his attending college and law school. He thanked Dr. Brodie for demonstrating to him and many other students who were awarded college scholarships by her, the sheer importance of community service and helping others in need. Mr. Coffey stated, "She didn't just give us the money, we had to earn it." He indicated that he and all other scholarship recipients were required to perform 400 hours of community service, primarily at the Robbins Village Hall, in conjunction with the acceptance and awarding of a full college scholarship. Notably, Attorney James Coffey, Jr. is the son of James Coffey, Sr., who served as a member of the Village Board of Trustees with the Honorable Mayor Brodie presiding. James Coffey, Sr. has been appointed by Mayor Tyrone Ward to serve again as a village trustee, this time serving out the remainder of the term of the trustee position vacated by Mayor Ward.

Mr. James Coffey, Jr. was followed in his presentation in honor of Dr. Brodie by two other scholarship recipients who also thanked Dr. Brodie for her generosity and the fine example that she set for aspiring youth. One of the speakers was a young woman who had become a teacher as a result of a scholarship provided by Dr. Brodie. She thanked Dr. Brodie for setting a fine example as a role model for her and for helping her to develop and maintain a good work ethic. A young man, who had just completed his studies with honors at Moraine Valley Community College, also took to the podium to thank Dr. Brodie for believing in him and giving him the chance to pursue his dreams. He commented, "I just want to let you know that your scholarship was not wasted." He continued on to let Dr. Brodie know that he had achieved honors in his coursework at Moraine Valley.

Mrs. Leota Murphy, a Robbins community activist, an organizer of the event, and a close neighbor of Dr. Brodie for over forty years, thanked Dr. Brodie for all she has done to help students, local residents, and people all across the country. She compared Dr. Brodie to an eagle. "The eagle is the most intelligent of all birds. The female eagle will fly into the storm when all other birds will fly away from the storm. You, Dr. Brodie, flew into the storms, and you weathered them." On behalf of the event organizing committee, Leota Murphy proudly presented Dr. Irene H. Brodie with a beautiful eagle sculpture made of crystal. Mrs. Murphy finalized her comments by stating, "Dr. Brodie, whenever you look at this eagle, remember that you weathered a lot of storms!"

As Dr. Brodie sat in honor at the event, soloist Delores Washington-Green sang as the band ever so gracefully played Dr. Brodie's favorite song: "Jesus is the Best Thing That Ever Happened to Me."

Governor Pat Quinn of the State of Illinois sent his heartfelt best wishes to Dr. Brodie. In a letter sent to mark and celebrate the occasion, Governor Quinn stated,

"As Governor, and on behalf of the people of the Land of Lincoln, it is my pleasure to congratulate you on your retirement as mayor of the Village of Robbins. During your time as mayor, you have provided Robbins, Illinois with your honorable and dedicated service. It is now time to look back and reflect on your many accomplishments.

The work that you have done for the Village of Robbins has undoubtedly created a lasting impact. Your professionalism has earned you the respect of your colleagues, and the mark that you leave behind will serve as a foundation for the future. Your life's commitment to public service has helped to make our state stronger and has served as an inspiration to your successors.

Most importantly, in all that you have done, your work ethic has exemplified the dedication to service, the citizens of this state deserve and expect. You have represented the State of Illinois admirably. Once again, congratulations. I wish you continued success in all your future endeavors. You have my respectful gratitude for your public service to the people of our state."

On Thursday, May 16, 2013 in Washington, D.C., Congressman Bobby L. Rush paid tribute to Dr. Irene H. Brodie by adopting a resolution in the United States House of Representatives recognizing and paying tribute to the contributions made by Dr. Brodie. As is also reflected in the Congressional Record of the 113th Congress (2013-2014), Congressman Bobby L. Rush of the First Congressional District in Illinois rose on the floor of the House of Representatives and stated,

"Mr. Speaker, I rise today to pay tribute to a dedicated public servant from my district, the Honorable Dr. Irene H. Brodie, mayor of the Village of Robbins. As Mayor Brodie retires after twenty-four years of service to the village, I wanted to take this opportunity to recognize her many achievements. Irene Brodie began her career in Robbins at Thomas J. Kellar Middle School where she worked alongside her husband, J. Edmon Brodie, who served as the school's principal. Through her hard work and diligence, she later became assistant principal at Turner Elementary School. In addition to her professional responsibilities, Brodie continued to be a loving and devoted wife and mother. While doing this, and in spite of her busy schedule, she earned her doctorate in education at Nova Southeastern University in Fort Lauderdale, Florida.

Now a recognized educator in the region, Dr. Brodie joined the staff of a small junior college that, at the time, had only a few buildings to accommodate its 12,000 students. After two years of serving as a professor, Dr. Brodie became the first African-American dean at Moraine Valley Community College. During her tenure, Moraine Valley grew to become the second largest community college in Illinois with a student population that now numbers well over 30,000.

Despite her having left the field, Dr. Brodie's dedication to education has never ceased. She has hired, financially supported, tutored, counseled, and graduated hundreds of residents from Robbins and the surrounding communities. Additionally, under her tutelage, the mayor's Scholarship Fund has funded tuition costs for hundreds of students through the years and her individual efforts have produced teachers, lawyers, doctors, engineers, and educators around the world. Her contributions to education were recognized when Moraine Valley named the "Dr. Irene H. Brodie Academic Skills Center" in her honor. This center serves as a critical area of academic enrichment for Moraine Valley students. During her tenure at Moraine Valley, Brodie also served as village clerk for the Village of Robbins for twelve years. Her service there led her to be recognized as a leader by a group of constituents who asked her to lead Robbins as its mayor. Her election as mayor marked her retirement from Moraine Valley and a shift in her career from educator to elected leader.

Mr. Speaker, throughout her career, Dr. Brodie has served in such leadership positions as vice president of the Illinois Municipal League, executive board member and assistant secretary of the National Conference of Black Mayors, and chair of the Education and Scholarship Committee for the National Conference of Black Mayors. Additionally, she has served as a member of the Metropolitan Mayors Caucus, numerous gubernatorial transition teams, various state and federal advisory boards, and as a member of President Clinton's Environmental Think-Tank Group.

In closing, Mr. Speaker, I would like to once again thank Mayor Brodie for her decades of service and congratulate her on her retirement."

The gala was a black-tie affair featuring live entertainment by a jazz band, Mr. Clark and Co. Attendees were led to a toast to the honoree by Mr.

Emmanuel "Manny" Williams, a prominent Robbins nightclub owner, and shortly after, guests dined on smoked salmon and beef roast with vegetables and au gratin potatoes.

At the end of a wonderful evening with family, friends, colleagues, and supporters, Dr. Brodie shared written words of acknowledgement with those in attendance.

"With a bit of sorrow, and a lot of excitement, I have looked forward to this day. I wish to formally express my sincere gratitude to all the persons that worked together to make this a wonderful night to remember. I remain grateful, however, for the opportunity to serve the residents of Robbins as Clerk for twelve years and as Mayor for twenty-four years. My thanks to all who served with me, it was our endeavor to make the Village of Robbins a better place for its residents. I wish the best of success to everyone who is remaining, and to those that are moving to new ground. Many of you have given me your friendship and well wishes, which transcend time. Thank you all for being here tonight and sharing this event with me."

Dr. Brodie, in ceremonial fashion, participated in the "Passing of the Gavel" to her successor, newly elected Mayor Tyrone Ward. Shortly afterwards, Dr. Irene H. Brodie was escorted to a limousine that awaited her as she set out on another journey—the return to her life as a regular person and a private citizen.

As a new day began on Saturday, May 18, 2013, as the sun shined on Robbins, and as the birds sang, the fresh smell of spring and the scents of many blossoms that come with it permeated the air, a small crowd gathered outside on the street corner of 135th Street and Springfield Avenue, directly across from the Delia Turner Elementary School, where Dr. Irene Brodie taught and served as assistant principal early on in her career. They were soon joined and greeted by Dr. Brodie, members of her family, and other well-wishers. They had all come together on this beautiful bright and sunny day to pay tribute once again to Dr. Brodie. By order of the Village of Robbins and its entire board of trustees, it was so ordered and resolved that in Robbins, 135th Street be re-named "Dr. Irene H. Brodie Way."

As Dr. Brodie unveiled the street sign that bears her name, in an honorable salutation by the people for all the hard work that she had done, all present for the ceremony erupted into a joyous applause. And so, just as it had been ordered by the Village Board of Trustees, it had been done. In Robbins, the stretch of 135th Street was now the Honorary Dr. Irene H. Brodie Way. Dr. Brodie's eldest sister, Reverend Evelyn Meachum of Kansas

THE INHERITANCE OF A DREAM

City, Missouri, led all who gathered on the corner of South Avers Avenue and Dr. Irene H. Brodie Way in prayer.

†

EPILOGUE

ROCK-IN-ROBBINS

"If people don't work together and put their differences aside, nothing will get accomplished. You get nowhere unless you do. My whole goal is to never divide but to unify. When you unify people, you get results."

—*Dr. Irene H. Brodie*

Upon her retirement from the office of mayor, Dr. Irene H. Brodie reclaimed her life as a regular person and a private citizen, a role that she had not played for the preceding thirty-six years of her life. She faced new challenges as she embraced this role, much the same way she faced challenges when she entered life in the public domain. She continues to rely on her abiding faith in God now, just as she had done so faithfully during the toughest times of her life. Dr. Irene H. Brodie now struggles with a debilitating health concern. The first signs of trouble were recognized several years ago while Mayor Brodie was in attendance at a National Conference of Black Mayors convention in Las Vegas, Nevada. Mayor Brodie collapsed at a conference seminar and was rushed to a Las Vegas hospital where she laid in a coma for several hours. She was officially diagnosed with a memory altering concern while serving her last term as mayor. In fact, her battle with the onset of this condition, midway through her sixth term as mayor, would ultimately serve as the deciding factor for her not seeking re-election.

It was her mayoral staff, colleagues, supporters, and personal friends who embraced and pushed her, as she had embraced and pushed them for so many years, that helped her successfully complete the duties discharged to her as mayor for the final few years of her last term. Dr. Brodie confronts her medical challenges just as she had her political opponents and life's other adversities in general – with fierce dedication, determination, and fight. Dr. Brodie's long-term memory has noticeably declined; remarkably, her resilience and determination for independence, as well as her spirit to fight adversity has remained at its strongest. She remains among the most dedicated members of her church, Great Hope M.B. Church, in Robbins. Dr. Brodie has been a member of Great Hope since her and her late husband, J.E. first moved to Robbins in the 1950s. Dr. Brodie has given an immeasurable amount of financial support to Great Hope, enabling the church to build a new church building. She has also contributed to many great causes supported by the church, including the installation of a modernized central air system for its main house of worship. No other member has been more loyal and giving to the causes of Great Hope Missionary Baptist Church than Sister Irene H. Brodie.

As Dr. Brodie embarked upon one of her life long endeavors, writing her memoir, the last year-and-a-half has presented her with medical challenges. This personal objective and literary work of Dr. Irene H. Brodie marks what is expected to be her last professional project. To those efforts, we can now declare "Mission Accomplished!" Due to health issues, Dr. Brodie has relocated, at least temporarily, to the Kansas City, Missouri area, not far away from the childhood farm home where she was raised, so that she can enjoy her retirement while under the care and watchful eye of her youngest sister, Bertha. In December 2014, just weeks before press time, Dr. Brodie's second eldest sister, Evelyn, passed away as a result of an apparent heart attack.

Just prior to Mayor Brodie completing her sixth and final term as mayor, one of her last orders of business along with supporting members of the Robbins Village Board of Trustees was to approve an agreement with a private mining company for the purpose of excavating the production of a major limestone mine recently discovered in Robbins. This find represents a major economic opportunity and promise for the Village of Robbins that is expected to greatly exceed any public works or economic project that the village has ever secured in its history, including the old waste-to-energy facility. The mining company estimates that the high quality grade of limestone is in such great abundance that production of the mine and quarry could continue for several decades with an annual production yielding tens of million dollars in limestone.

Not only would the Village of Robbins stand to gain millions of dollars in annual revenue from its production agreement with the mining company, but many of the residents of the village whose homes and businesses are located above vast deposits of limestone, stand to gain economic benefits as well for their rights to the important mineral-laden rock. By all serious accounts, this vast discovery of this precious mineral that lies beneath in the bedrock of much of the land covering the Village of Robbins is estimated to exceed $1 billion in value. Never in the history of Robbins, a town that has often been cited as one of the poorest cities in Illinois and the nation, has such an economic opportunity arisen. It was one of Mayor Brodie's last official acts while in office—entering into a multimillion dollar operating agreement, which is anticipated to bring in millions of dollars in revenue for the Village of Robbins, and is expected to provide Robbins with an unprecedented surplus in operating revenue which will lead to a budget surplus.

So, the Village of Robbins, under the new leadership of Mayor Tyrone Ward, a one-time political foe and nemesis of Mayor Brodie, is poised to reap the financial rewards from projects put in place by Mayor Brodie during her years of service. As it was Mayor Brodie's commitment upon first being elected to serve as mayor to help Robbins grow and develop economically, in this regard, we can now declare that her goal was further achieved with the execution of the mining agreement. Subsequently, however, the agreement would be renegotiated and amended by Mayor Tyrone Ward and his administration.

A litmus test that is often applied to measure a public servant's progress and success while in office is applied simply by answering the question: "Are you better off today than when she or he first took office?" It is apparent that the answer as it applied to Mayor Irene H. Brodie is "Yes." The people of the Village of Robbins have progressed and have come a long way since Dr. Brodie was first elected and sworn-in as mayor in 1989. Mayor Brodie has brought integrity and stability back to the village government of Robbins.

Moraine Valley Community College, since its inception in the 1960s has now grown to become the second largest community college in the State of Illinois. In honor of Dr. Brodie, who served the college loyally since it first opened its doors to students, the college has named a section of its "B-wing" in honor of Dr. Brodie and her years of dedicated service. The Dr. Irene H. Brodie Academic Skills Center is a vital part of the college's efforts to attract students who may be disadvantaged and academically challenged, and to prepare them with a foundation to attain a higher level of quality education. The Dr. Irene H. Brodie Academic Skills Center continues to serve as a gateway to quality education for Robbins students and disadvantaged students from throughout the South Chicagoland Region and across the world. Helping to provide access to a quality and affordable education is what Dr. Brodie dedicated much of her life to.

The Village of Robbins, Illinois continues its struggle to maintain its independence as a municipality and to harness its financial resources to induce economic development and growth. In June 2014, Cook County Sheriff Tom Dart conducted an investigation relating to the agreement entered into between the Village of Robbins and ALM Resources, LLC, the lead developer of the proposed limestone mine and quarry. Sheriff Dart demanded that the agreement between the Village of Robbins and ALM be renegotiated. Sheriff Dart's investigation concluded that the residents of Robbins had not been included in the process as much as they should have been and, therefore, some of their rights as citizens may have been jeopardized. The sheriff's investigation also concluded that the Village of Robbins, under the current agreement, would not receive a fair share of the profits derived from the operations of the proposed mine and quarry.

In addition, adding to the cloud of suspicion relating to the fairness and transparency of the agreement between the Village of Robbins and ALM Resources, LLC. Sheriff Tom Dart's investigation uncovered that former Trustee Shantiel X. Simon, who was a candidate for mayor of the Village of Robbins at the time, had accepted approximately $4,800 in campaign contributions from the limestone mine developer, ALM Resources, and its president, James Louthen. According to Mr. Louthen, the contributions were made to Trustee Simon's campaign for mayor by several companies controlled by either Louthen directly or indirectly through ALM Resources, LLC which was also under the control of Louthen.

The initial agreement between the Village of Robbins and ALM Resources received unanimous approval by the Village Board of Trustees, including Mayor-Elect Tyrone Ward. The terms of the agreement were in large part negotiated by the Robbins Village Board of Trustees and then-village administrator, Napoleon Haney. Mayor Brodie supported their efforts and executed the agreement on behalf of the Village of Robbins. However, since that time and upon the urging of Cook County Sheriff Tom Dart, the agreement is expected to be renegotiated by Mayor Brodie's successor, Mayor Tyrone Ward and the current Village Board of Trustees in order to assure complete fairness, transparency, and terms of agreement that will be the absolute best, economically, for Robbins and all of its residents.

Since Mayor Brodie's retirement from office, some opponents of the limestone mine and quarry project, including a few members of the local press, have attempted to make her the convenient scapegoat for the approval of the agreement between the Village of Robbins and the project's lead developer, ALM Resources, LLC. Those who make such irresponsible and, in some cases, outright reckless assertions, are completely blind as to how the apparatus of municipal government works. Mayor Brodie could not have signed a proposal into law, unless it was first passed by the Village Board of Trustees. In this case, the proposal received the unanimous vote of all six members of the Village

Board of Trustees, including Mayor-Elect Tyrone Ward. When a proposal is passed by a unanimous vote comprised of a supermajority of the legislative body of a municipal government, even if the mayor were to choose to veto the proposal, the Village Board of Trustees would have the power to override such a veto. So, the assertion that former Mayor Brodie is solely responsible for approving the proposal between the village and developers of the limestone mine and quarry is disingenuous, to say the least.

With the discovery of this vast mine of limestone buried beneath the bedrock of much of the land covering the Village of Robbins, the village government and its residents have an opportunity like never before to harness the financial resources that could be derived from the mineral-laden rock and use the financial gains to build a more prosperous future for the village and its residents. Robbins now has the opportunity that it has longed for since its inception, to strengthen and maintain its independence as a municipality, and to prosper and shine as bright as or brighter than all of its neighboring communities.

APPENDIX A

A LETTER FROM JERAYE

Appendix courtesy of Dr. Irene H. Brodie

Oct. 13, 1974

Dear Momsy,

Here I sit at 11:45 thinking of you. I know that you'd probably rather hear that from some filthy rich, 50-year-old, good-looking, unmarried doctor, but unfortunately it's only I. I'm not sleepy yet probably because I've had a nap. I think that I'll work on my religion paper due Fri. which I'll bring home for help in typing if I come Wednes.

I thought that I'd add this letter to your neat card to let you know that I've broken the right lens in one pair of glasses. It fell out of the frame. It was the one that was broken. I've got the other pair, but I'm taking these to Gailey's (remember the $103 bill?) tomorrow when I take my shoes to be repaired. So chalk up another set of bills.

I'm not upset about my eye ointment and drops. I've bought the ointment already and the drops are on the counter at Osco's downtown. So if I wasn't clear when talking to you on the phone because I'd just awakened from the phone ringing, that's what I'd meant to explain to you.

This room is still burning up. I sleep with the curtains open on Susie's (the head resident) suggestion. It serves 2 purposes:1)cools the room and 2)gives me light in the room so I don't sleep with the light on.

That Lori is a mess. I can't wait to see her again.

I plan to send Sue (La Gene) a card tomorrow.

How is Aunt Pat's father? Tell her that I asked about him and her.

For dinner I've had a chicken dinner from across the street, then later went to McDonald's for a Big Mac, fries, and a coke. I ate the whole thing--chicken dinner right down to the bun and honey. I know that it's mostly junk, but the purpose today was to stuff and try to gain weight.

Get me a stereo needle and I'll

Love you lots,
Stuffy
Stuff

You're part of my life
the NICEST part

145

APPENDIX B

ILLINOIS
HOUSE RESOLUTION
No. 148

Appendix courtesy of Dr. Irene H. Brodie

STATE OF ILLINOIS
HOUSE OF REPRESENTATIVES
98TH GENERAL ASSEMBLY

◆

HOUSE RESOLUTION NO. 148
OFFERED BY REPRESENTATIVE ROBERT RITA

WHEREAS, The members of the Illinois House of Representatives are pleased to honor Dr. Irene H. Brodie, mayor of the Village of Robbins, as as retires after 24 years; and

WHEREAS, Mayor Brodie is the current, longest-serving, female, African-American mayor in the nation; her reign as mayor saw improvements in the water and sewer systems, roads and transportation, code enforcement, economic development, grant procurement, land acquisition, residential development, and public safety; and

WHEREAS, Mayor Brodie's 36-year tenure in government consists of 12 years as municipal clerk for the Village of Robbins and 24 years as the mayor; she is a longtime educator and administrator, having taught in school districts 143 1/2 and 218 and achieving the position of dean at Moraine Valley Community College; she spent 32 years of service to Moraine Valley and upon her retirement a section of Building-B was named the "Dr. Irene H. Brodie Academic Skills Center"; and

WHEREAS, Mayor Brodie's most noteworthy accomplishment is her scholarship program; it has funded the tuition costs for hundreds of students throughout the years and her individual efforts have produced teachers, lawyers, doctors, engineers, and educators around the globe; she has hired, financially supported, tutored, counseled, and graduated hundreds of residents from Robbins and the surrounding communities; and

WHEREAS, Mayor Brodie has a history of service in many areas; she was the vice-president of the Illinois Municipal League, executive board member and assistant secretary of the National Conference of Black Mayors, and the chair of the Education Committee and Scholarship Committee for the National Conference of Black Mayors; she has been appointed to numerous gubernatorial transition teams and has been on various State and federal advisory boards; she was a member of the Metropolitan Mayors Caucus under Mayor Richard Daley, served on President Clinton's environmental think-tank group, and was a guest lecturer at the Harvard University Graduate School of Business; and

WHEREAS, Mayor Brodie is married to J. Edmon Brodie and they have one child, Jeraye E. Brodie; therefore, be it

RESOLVED, BY THE HOUSE OF REPRESENTATIVES OF THE NINETY-EIGHTH GENERAL ASSEMBLY OF THE STATE OF ILLINOIS, that we honor Mayor Irene Brodie as she retires as mayor of Robbins, thank her for her years of service to the community, and wish her well in all her future endeavours; and be it further

RESOLVED, That a suitable copy of this resolution be presented to Mayor Irene Brodie as an expression of our esteem and respect.

Adopted by the House of Representatives on March 13, 2013.

TIMOTHY D. MAPES
CLERK OF THE HOUSE

MICHAEL J. MADIGAN
SPEAKER OF THE HOUSE

APPENDIX C

A LETTER FROM FORMER GOV. JIM EDGAR

Appendix courtesy of Dr. Irene H. Brodie

STATE OF ILLINOIS

OFFICE OF THE GOVERNOR

CHICAGO 60601

JIM EDGAR
GOVERNOR

March 21, 1994

Honorable Irene Brodie, Ph.D.
Village President
Village of Robbins
3327 West 137th Street
Robbins, IL 60472

Dear Irene:

As Governor of the State of Illinois, I am proud to congratulate you for your dedication and hard work as the Village President of Robbins.

It is through this dedication and hard work that you are being honored by Harvard University. Addressing the faculty and students of Harvard's Business School is quite an accomplishment.

For 75 years, the Village of Robbins has struggled against an economic deficit. Under your strong leadership and guidance, however, the picture has changed. Where once there was poverty and despair, Robbins is seeing opportunity and hope. Your determination has been key to reversing nearly a century of economic hardship, and I commend you for this monumental accomplishment. It is no wonder such a prestigious institution of learning has extended you an invitation.

On behalf of the citizens of Illinois, we are very proud of you.

Sincerely,

Jim Edgar
GOVERNOR

JE:sl

APPENDIX D

MAYOR BRODIE'S
LETTER TO THE EDITOR

Appendix courtesy of Dr. Irene H. Brodie

Chicago Tribune | **Letters to the Editor**
March 22, 1996

"Governor Jim Edgar's recent action on the Retail Rate Law has struck a blow so devastating, the repercussions will reverberate for years. It is unconscionable that the Robbins trash-to-energy and the Ford Heights tire-to-energy plants will not receive incentives from the state but that landfills have been grandfathered in to receive those same payments.

By excluding two of its poorest communities, the state has been successful in guaranteeing that benefits desperately needed for economic development will be given freely to wealthy landfill corporations. The unfairness is beyond belief. To my community, the most devastating aspect of this action is the loss of revenue. We worked for the development of this state-of-the-art recycling and waste-disposal facility just as hard as others who have already received state assistance, and who worked much less for their projects. But to maintain Republican control of both houses of the legislature, the governor made Robbins a sacrificial lamb.

A second concern is that investors will not trust the State of Illinois to keep its word. The governor's action has now set the stage for a potential bond default—the third largest in U.S. history. I am also saddened for the people of the South and Southwest Suburbs, who have been fed inaccurate information by their state legislators—all for the sake of re-election. These legislators can't win elections on merit so they resort to creating issues involving communities lacking political clout.

One wonders what is in store for Illinois if this action is precedent for how the state will treat development in the future. Or is it just in Robbins that economic development is viewed as a pariah?"

—Mayor Irene H. Brodie

APPENDIX E

A LETTER FROM
DR. VERNON O. CRAWLEY

Appendix courtesy of Dr. Irene H. Brodie

Moraine Valley
Community College

May 20, 1998

Irene Brodie
Moraine Valley Community College
Palos Hills, IL 60465

Dear Irene:

During the recent Recognition Dinner, it gave me great pleasure to recognize publicly all the good work you do on behalf of Moraine Valley Community College. Your leadership, dedication and commitment to the college are the foundation for our success. With your help, we are able to reach out to more students, provide needed services, and continue our tradition of offering quality education to all who have a desire to learn.

I have enclosed a photograph taken of you receiving your award. I hope it serves as a constant reminder of our appreciation of your exemplary service. On behalf of the entire college community, I want to express my sincere appreciation for your dedication and service to Moraine Valley.

Sincerely,

Vernon O. Crawley
President

lfn
Enclosure

10900 South 88th Avenue • Palos Hills, Illinois 60465-0937

APPENDIX F

A CERTIFICATE OF
AWARD FROM UNCF

Appendix courtesy of Dr. Irene H. Brodie

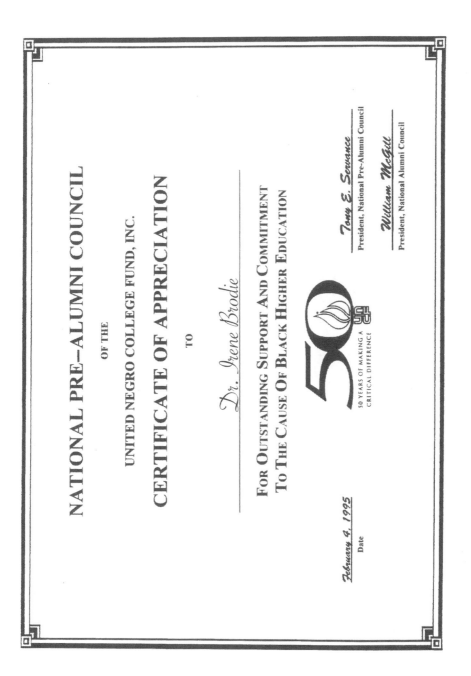

NATIONAL PRE–ALUMNI COUNCIL

OF THE

UNITED NEGRO COLLEGE FUND, INC.

CERTIFICATE OF APPRECIATION

TO

Dr. Irene Brodie

FOR OUTSTANDING SUPPORT AND COMMITMENT
TO THE CAUSE OF BLACK HIGHER EDUCATION

50 YEARS OF MAKING A
CRITICAL DIFFERENCE

Tony E. Sewance
President, National Pre–Alumni Council

William McGill
President, National Alumni Council

February 4, 1995
Date

APPENDIX G

MAYOR BRODIE'S
LIST OF PERSONNEL
(1989-2013)

Data included herein compiled and
provided by Robbins History Museum

Village of Robbins, Illinois
MAYOR IRENE H. BRODIE'S HISTORIC
SIX-TERM ADMINISTRATION
(1989-2013) 24 YEARS
Roster of Elected and Appointed officials and other administrative department
heads and Supervisory employees who served in the six-term administration of
Mayor Irene H. Brodie. (1 Term = 4 years)

Mayor Brodie's 1st Term (1989-93)

Irene H. Brodie	Mayor	Unity Party
Tyrone Haymore	Clerk	Unity Party
Willie E. Carter	Trustee	Unity Party
Richard Williams	Trustee	Unity Party
Palma James	Trustee	Unity Party
Marvin C. Chandler	Trustee (1991)	Better Government Party
Paul Rayon	Trustee (1991)	Better Government Party
Hearthel Johnson	Trustee (1991)	Better Government Party

(Mayor Brodie's 2nd Term) 1993-97

Irene H. Brodie	Mayor	Unity Party
Tyrone Haymore	Clerk	Unity Party
Willie E. Carter	Trustee	Unity Party
Richard Williams	Trustee	Unity Party
Palma James	Trustee	Unity Party
David Bryant	Trustee (1995)	Unity Party
Gregory Wright	Trustee (1995)	Unity Party
James E. Coffey	Trustee (1995)	Unity Party

(Mayor Brodie's 3rd Term) 1997-01

Irene H. Brodie	Mayor	Unity Party
Palma James	Trustee	Unity Party
Willie E. Carter	Trustee	Unity Party
Richard Williams	Trustee	Unity Party
Lynnie Johnson	Trustee	Unity Party
Gregory Wright	Trustee (1999)	Unity Party
James E. Coffey	Trustee (1999)	Unity Party

Adele Sharp   Trustee (1999) Unity Party

(Mayor Brodie's 4th Term) 2001-05

Irene H. Brodie	Mayor	Unity Party
Palma James	Trustee	Unity Party
Willie E. Carter	Trustee	Unity Party
Richard Williams	Trustee	Unity Party
Lynnie Johnson	Trustee	Unity Party
Gregory Wright	Trustee (2003)	Unity Party
James E. Coffey	Trustee (2003)	Unity Party
Adele Sharp	Trustee (2003)	Unity Party

(Mayor Brodie's 5th Term) 2005-09

Irene H. Brodie	Mayor	Unity Party
Pamela M. Bradley	Clerk	Independent
Willie E. Carter	Trustee	Unity Party
Richard Williams	Trustee	Unity Party
Chanel Kelley	Trustee	Unity Party
Tyrone Haymore	Trustee (2007)	Independent
Shantiel X. Simon	Trustee (2007)	Independent
Tyrone Ward	Trustee (2007)	Independent

(Mayor Brodie's 6th Term) 2009-13

Irene H. Brodie	Mayor	Unity Party
Pamela M. Bradley	Clerk	Independent
Willie E. Carter	Trustee	Unity Party
Richard Williams	Trustee	Unity Party
Chanel Kelley	Trustee	Unity Party
Tyrone Haymore	Trustee (2011)	Independent
Shantiel X. Simon	Trustee (2011)	Independent
Lynnie Johnson	Trustee (2011)	Independent

Village Treasurers:

1. James Jackson, Jr.   CPA (Special Interim-Village Treasurer)
   Owner of Jackson Liquor Store
2. Marsha Bond   CPA

3. Ludella Lewis   CPA
4. Jeanette Ray
5. Ora Leach
6. Margaret Newell

Village Collectors:
1. James Kimbrough
2. Margaret Newell
3. Palma James   CLERK (Part Time)

Village Auditors:
1. Greg Kenner   CPA w/John E. Wilson & Assoc.
2. Ed Wright, (Rev.)   CPA (Part Time)
3. Kevin Carter (Part Time)
4. Brown & Mayer
5. Letke & Associates   CPA

Accounts Payable Clerks:
1. Marlene Hunter
2. Linda Cologne-Hunt
3. Sherry Thomas

Personnel/Payroll/Human Resources Department:
1. Sandra Lee   PAYROLL CLERK
2. Gregory Wright   PERSONNEL DIRECTOR
3. Peggy Collier   HUMAN RESOURCES DIRECTOR

Executive Secretaries To Mayor Brodie:
1. Mary Jones
2. Marlene Hunter (Mother of Police Chief James Parks II)
3. Sylvia Parham
4. Jamaico Mcgee
5. Lillie Crockling

Village Attorneys:
1. Burton Oldelson and Mark Sterk,
   Odelson & Sterk Law Firm of Evergreen Park, Illinois

2. Swanson & Brown Law Firm

Village Administrators:
1. Ernestine Berry-Beck Fulgham
2. Beverly Gavin
3. Napoleon Haney

Village Planners:
1. Ernestine Berry-Beck Fulgham
2. Phil Simon
3. Napoleon Haney
4. Sylvia Parham
5. Sharon Armwood-Boyd

Police & Fire Commission Board:
(Three Members Appointed by Mayor Brodie)
1. Leonard "Snookie" Wallace
2. Lillian Dunn-Barker
3. Jesse Shears
4. James Collier

Police Chiefs: Appointed by Mayor Brodie
1. James Parks II
2. Johnny Holmes
3. Jerome Guinn

Police Pension Fund Board:
(Two Members Appointed by Mayor Brodie)
1. Jerome Guinn
2. Leonard Boston
3. Robert Warren
4. Marshawn Henderson
5. Margaret Newell   Treasurer

Fire Chiefs: (Appointed by Mayor Brodie)
1. Charles Lloyd

Firemen's Pension Fund Board:
(Two Members Appointed by Mayor Brodie)
1. Irene H. Brodie   MAYOR
2. Palma James   CLERK
3. Margaret Newell   TREASURER
4. Charles Lloyd

Water Department:
1. Yvonne Pritchett, WATER DEPARTMENT SUPERVISOR

Debra Peterson	CLERK
Carman Dunlap	CLERK
Beverly Martin	CLERK

2. Denise Allen-Moore,
   WATER DEPARTMENT SUPERVISOR (22 YRS BEGINNING 5/26/1989-2011)

Michelle Moody	CLERK
Kathy Johnson	CLERK
Loralene Colquitt	CLERK
Karla Burden	CLERK
Teleda Ellis	CLERK
Lydia Craig	CLERK
Sharon Palmer	CLERK
Tracey Byrd	CLERK

3. Lillian Dunn-Barker, WATER DEPARTMENT SUPERVISOR

Sally Johnson	CLERK
Lyniece Toliver	CLERK
Denise Fisher	CLERK

Building Department
1. Fred Jefferson   BUILDING COMMISSIONER
2. Henry Short   BUILDING COMMISSIONER
3. Derrick Carter (Rev.)   BUILDING COMMISSIONER

4. Jeffery BoBo (Rev.)	BUILDING COMMISSIONER
5. Royce Coleman	BUILDING COMMISSIONER
Eddie Rhodes	ASSISTANT BUILDING COMMISSIONER
Leota Murphy	FIRST CODE ENFORCEMENT COMMISSIONER 2001
	HEALTH INSPECTOR
Anthony Craig	ASSISTANT CODE ENFORCEMENT OFFICER
Robert ReChord	ELECTRICAL INSPECTOR
Derrick Carter (Rev.)	ELECTRICAL INSPECTOR
Lewis Richmond	ELECTRICAL INSPECTOR
William Dowdy	PLUMBING INSPECTOR
Leroy Gill	PLUMBING INSPECTOR
Caleb Johnson,	HEALTH INSPECTOR
Shirley Howard, RN, MS	HEALTH INSPECTOR
Franklin Jenkins	CHIEF HEALTH INSPECTOR

Building Department Administrative Assistants:
1. Audrey Moody
2. Vanessa Banks
3. Jackie Carter
4. Inella Campbell
5. Ms. Peterson
6. Theresa Sims
7. Jamaico Mcgee
8. Vielka Sterling

Planning Commission Board Chairman:
1. Ulysses Jones

Zoning Board Chairman:
1. Jimmy Martin

Public Works Directors:
1. Freddie Davis
2. Bernard Ward
3. Mike Wilson

Maintenance Engineers:
1. Esdra Hays
2. Ed Lindsey
3. Charles Calhoun
4. Michael Braswell
5. Marshawn Porter
6. Marvin Jones
7. Kevin Dillard

Flea Market Supervisors/Managers:
1. Julius Howe
2. Houston Fuller
3. Jamaico Mcgee

Robbins Cable TV Operators:
1. Tyrone Haymore
2. Edward "Ed" Lindsey
3. Napoleon Haney
4. Sherry Thomas

Village Deputy-Clerks:
1. Louise Roster (CLERK IRENE BRODIE)
2. Karen Rollins (CLERK IRENE BRODIE)
3. Beverly Martin-Anderson (CLERK IRENE BRODIE)
4. Maple Spearmon (CLERK IRENE BRODIE)
5. Love Barnes (CLERK IRENE BRODIE)
6. Maude Johnson (CLERK IRENE BRODIE)
7. Delean Dozier-Fuller (CLERK IRENE BRODIE)
8. Sharon Wallace (CLERK IRENE BRODIE)
9. Michelle Moody (MAYOR IRENE BRODIE)
10. Patricia Simmons (MAYOR IRENE BRODIE)

ROBBINS POLICE DEPARTMENT

The following represents a list of Robbins Police Officers,
Dispatchers, Clerks, and Secretaries who served in the department during the
historic six-term administration of Mayor Irene H. Brodie.

Leonard Boston
Davis Bryant
Benjamin Clark
Charles Clark   OFFICER, POLICE CHIEF
Raymond Clark
Sam Coleman
Golden Duer
Charles Foster
Don Grayson
Jerome Guinn   OFFICER, CAPTAIN, POLICE CHIEF
Charles Harris
Marshawn Henderson
Williams Hooks
Johnny Holmes   OFFICER, POLICE CHIEF
Robert Holloway
Romel Jamison
Michael Kemp
Dion Kimble
Anthony Koetzle
Harold Kohn
Julius Lowe
Devell Mathis
James Moore Jr.
Lawrence Moore
Frederick Pennix, Sr.   OFFICER, SGT. POLICE CHIEF
Sol Veal
Warren, Robert   OFFICER, CAPTAIN, SPECIAL SECURITY TO MAYOR
Carl Williams   OFFICER, SERGEANT, POLICE CHIEF
Ronald Wolfolk

Female Police Officers/Matrons:
Beatrice Darden
Benita Clerk
Geraldine Smith

Police Dispatchers/Clerks/Secretaries:
Beverly Martin
Handy, Artis
James Kimbrough
Cherita Moore
Karen Gray
Angle Carpenter
Johnnie Bradley
Lisa Plummerel
Tawasha Walker

Chaplans of Robbins Police Deptartment

Reverend Johnny Rupert	CHAPLAN
Reverend James Parks Sr.	CHAPLAN
Reverend David Leach	CHAPLAN, PERSONAL SECURITY FOR MAYOR

ROBBINS FIRE DEPARTMENT

The following represents a list of Robbins Firefighters who were in
service during the historic six-term administration of Mayor Irene H. Brodie.

Charles B. Lloyd Sr.	FT-FIRE CHIEF
Wesley Marvel	FT-DEPUTY CHIEF
Donald Rush	FT-DEPUTY CHIEF
Nicholas Malley	FT-DEPUTY CHIEF
Nicholas Sykes	FT-CAPTAIN
Jasund Norman	CAPTAIN
Donald Jimerson	PT-LIEUTENANT
Robert Davis	PT-LIEUTENANT
Steve Wilson	FT-LIEUTENANT
Charles Johnson	FT-ENGINEER

Raymond Anderson	FT-ENGINEER
Jason Starosta	P.O.C.-ENGINEER
Charles Smith	PT-ENGINEER
Anton Sykes	PT-ENGINEER
Songo Bailey	PT-ENGINEER
Wes Thomas	P.O.C.-FIREFIGHTER
Howard Fisher	P.O.C.-FIREFIGHTER
Steve Allen	PT-FIREFIGHTER
Martin Sobanski	PT-FIREFIGHTER
Vance Woods	P.O.C.-FIREFIGHTER
Gervaise Porter	P.O.C.-FIREFIGHTER
*Danita Reese	P.O.C.-FIREFIGHTER
*Andranique Mickens	P.O.C.-FIREFIGHTER
*Juanita Smith	FIREFIGHTER
*Consuela Roberts	FIREFIGHTER
Willie McCloud	P.O.C.-FIREFIGHTER
Bernard Butler	P.O.C.-FIREFIGHTER
Jeffrey Brewer	P.O.C.-FIREFIGHTER
Malante Jones	P.O.C.-FIREFIGHTER
D. Patterson	P.O.C.-FIREFIGHTER

Cadets:
Dai'Jerne Slater
Raymond Anderson, Jr.
Turon Windham
Dantzler Newell III
Torriano Russell
Lawrence Mullins
Dai'Treona Doty

FT= Full Time PT= Part Time
P.O.C.= Paid On Call Vol.= Volunteer * = Female

Former Robbins Firefighters who served during
Mayor Irene H. Brodie's historic six-term administration

Earl Abercrombie
Songo Bailey
James Bond
Kevin Bond
David Bridgewater
Henry Brown
William Brown
Quentin Butler
Irving Carter
Donald Carter, Jr.
Albert Carter, Jr.
Mark Clark
Daniel Clayton, Jr.
Daniel Clayton, Sr.
Denard Clement
Walker Clemons
Anthony Craig
Marcus Curd
Robert Dampler
William Driskell
Juan Ellis
Jimmie Fields
Joe Guarascio
David Hicks (DayDay)
Lawrence Hobson
Michael Hobson
Brandon Hughes
Matthew Jiggets
Bradley Johnson
Michael Jones
Cedell Jones, Sr.
Wilson Jordan, III
Joe Laury
Kevin Clayton
Charles Lloyd, Jr.
Charles Lloyd, Sr.
Robert Lobianco
Robert Malone
Mokadi Manson
Harold Martin
Robert Martin
Carlee Martin, Jr.

Calvin Mays
Gerald McCline
Gavin McCoy, Sr.
Noble McDowell, Jr.
Marcus McFadden
W. McNairy
Earl Mims
Dwight Moore
Jeffery Nailon
Brian Nape
Melvin Ousley
Paul Parenti
Robert Perkins
Jerry Phillips
Robert Rapka
Kenneth Ray
Darrell Reeder
Michael Reid
Russell Reid
Robert Rollins
Alfred Scott
Glenn Scott
Steven Serviss
Berttron Shaw
Brian Shaw
Jesse Shores
Charles Smith
Leon Smith
Mickil Smith
Randy Starosta
Will Steppes
Vincent Stevens
Laverne Steward
Sam Syas
Kenneth Wayne
Jimmie Webb
Brandon Williams
Morry Williams
Terry Young

NOTES

PROLOGUE: CIVIL RIGHTS AND QUALITY EDUCATION

1. *Encyclopedia Britannica Online*, s.v. "Twenty-fourth Amendment," accessed January 02, 2015, http://www.britannica.com/EBchecked/topic/611014/Twenty-fourth Amendment.
2. *Encyclopedia Britannica Online*, s.v. "Jim Crow law," accessed January 02, 2015, http://www.britannica.com/EBchecked/topic/303897/Jim-Crow-law.
3. Evers, Charles and Szanton, Andrew, "Have No Fear: The Charles Evers Story, 1996.
4. Wolf, Wayne L., The Gin Bottle Riot of 1964: Harvey and Dixmoor in Flames. 1977.
5. WTTW Online, "Power, Politics, & Pride: Dr. King's Chicago Crusade," accessed on January 02, 2015, http://www.wttw.com/main,taf?p=76,4,5,7.

CHAPTER 5: HISTORIC ROBBINS, ILLINOIS

1. Bonnie Miller Rubin, "Town never forgets its heritage," *Chicago Tribune*, July 2, 1994.
2. "History of Robbins," Wikipedia, July 15, 2012, http://en.wikipedia.org/wiki/Robbins,_Illinois.
3. Thomas J. Kellar, "History of Robbins, Illinois," December 17, 1921, https://edocs.uis.edu/mleon1/www/Texts/village.htm, July 15, 20112.
4. "Village of Robbins…A community with a vision," July 15, 2012, http://www.robbins-il.com/.
5. Tyrone Haymore, "Historic Robbins, Illinois," September 2008.
6. Ayele Bekerie, "Ethiopia & Black America: The Forgotten Story of Melaku & Robinson," News Room, August 24, 2008.
7. Dennis Nishi, "*Star Trek's* Nichelle Nichols on How Martin Luther King Jr. Changed Her Life" *Wall Street Journal*, January 17, 2011.

CHAPTER 7: MORAINE VALLEY

1. Helen B. Nebe, "Birth of a junior college," August 7, 1967.
2. "Region V Benefactor to Moraine Valley Community College," *CRD Benefactor Awards Banquet Program*, November 22, 2002.

CHAPTER 8: HIDDEN IN PLAIN SIGHT
1. *Samuel Coleman v. Marion Smith, Gordon Frierson, and Village of Robbins.* U.S. Court of Appeals, Seventh Circuit. Nos. 85-1769, 85-1770, 85-3081, and 85-3084. January 20, 1987.

CHAPTER 9: VILLAGE CLERK YEARS
1. Kelly Flores, "Robbins clerk cries foul," *Southtown Economist,* March 14, 1989.

CHAPTER 11: LADY B
1. Tonita R. Cheatham, "Mayor Assesses Leadership Progress," *South-Suburban Citizen,* September 26-29, 1991.
2. Beth Anne Janicki, "What is home rule?" Illinois Municipal League

CHAPTER 13: THE BURNER WARS
1. Margaret Ann Charles and Jonathan V.L. Kiser, "Waste-to-Energy: Benefits Beyond Waste Disposal," *Solid Waste Technologies / 1995 Industry Sourcebook,* 1995.
2. Bill Schwingel, "Robbins eyes burner TIF plan…," *The Star,* July 3, 1994.
3. Jeff Leitner, "Robbins mayor makes plea for Naper garbage," *The Naperville Sun,* November 26, 1995.

CHAPTER 14: ENVIRONMENTAL RACISM v. ECONOMIC OPPORTUNITY
1. Jim Ritter, "Incinerator Subsidy Ends; Firms Cry Foul," *Chicago Sun-Times,* March 15, 1996.
2. James Dudlicek, "Burner foes gain Dem allies in state repeal fight…," *The Regional News,* January 11, 1996.
3. Lynnie Johnson, "Angry with Edgar," *Daily Southtown,* April 9, 1996.
4. David Schoenbrod, "Environmental 'Injustice' Is About Politics, Not Racism," *The Wall Street Journal,* February 23, 1994.
5. Jim Ritter, "Waste Study Finds No Racism in Siting," *Chicago Sun-Times,* October 25, 1994.
6. Pamela Cytrynbaum, "Robbins mayor tries to stay the course with incinerator," *Chicago Tribune,* January 26, 1996
7. Joe Robertson, "Up in smoke?" *Sunday Southtown,* January 21, 1996.
8. Editorial, "Company knew project's risks," *The Beverly Review,* April 3, 1996.
9. Editorial, "The burner wars," *The Star,* January 11, 1996.

CHAPTER 15: STRANGE BEDFELLOWS

1. Tom Rybarczyk, "Dolton hires mayor's brother to fight graft," *Chicago Tribune,* May 05, 2006.
2. Rick Pearson and Stacy St. Clair, "William "Bill" Shaw: 1937-2008," *Chicago Tribune,* November 28, 2008.
3. Ben Joravsky, "The Shaw Brothers: An Appreciation," *Chicago Reader,* December 18, 2008.

CHAPTER 16: BOSS LADY

1. Sunya Walls, "Irene Brodie: Staying Put To Make A Difference," *South Suburban Citizen,* February 9, 1995.
2. Phil Rockrohr, "Robbins' Brodie wins raves at Harvard," *The Star,* June 5, 1994.
3. Phil Rockrohr, "Robbins' Brodie dazzles Harvard students," *The Star,* June 5, 1994.
4. Sarah Karp, "Robbins weighs home rule," *Daily Southtown,* January 8, 1998.

CHAPTER 17: REALIZING THE DREAM

1. Editorial, "A rebirth in Robbins," *Chicago Sun-Times,* October 24, 1997
2. M.L. Elrick, "Robbins gets gift from House," *Daily Southtown,* October 10, 1997.
3. Basil Talbott, "Robbins mayor wins battle to erase debt," *Chicago Sun-Times,* October 20, 1997.
4. Jennifer Delgado, "Suburbs planning for casino cash," *Chicago Tribune,* July 15, 2011.

CHAPTER 20: R.P.D. BLUES

1. Casey Toner, "Ex-police chief who retired after two DUIs still getting paid," *Southtown Star,* March 23, 2013.
2. Angie Leventis Lourgos, "Robbins police chief fired in wake of state investigation," *Chicago Tribune,* November 22, 2013.
3. Bryan Smith, "The Trouble with Robbins," *Chicago* magazine, December 2014.

CHAPTER 22: HONORING A GREAT LADY

1. "Honoring A Great Lady," *Program,* May 17, 2013.

EPILOGUE: ROCK-IN-ROBBINS

1. Casey Toner, "Massive quarry, underground limestone mine planned in

Robbins," *Southtown Star,* October 11, 2013.

2.   Bryan Smith, "The Trouble with Robbins," *Chicago* magazine, December 2014.

INDEX

INDEX

ABOUT THE AUTHORS

DR. IRENE H. BRODIE

Dr. Irene H. Brodie is a retired government official and leading educator. She served as clerk of the Village of Robbins, Illinois, for twelve years and became the first woman elected mayor of the historic village, where she served an unprecedented six consecutive four-year terms. She served as Dean of Educational Development at Moraine Valley Community College and founded The J.E. and Jeraye E. Brodie Memorial Scholarship Fund, that has helped a countless number of students pursue their dreams of attending college. An honoree of the White House and President Barack Obama in 2012 for her contributions to humanity, Dr. Brodie temporarily resides in the Kansas City, Missouri area, while maintaining her permanent residence in Robbins, Illinois.

VINCENT WILLIAMS

Vincent Williams is an author and publisher. He attended the University of Illinois at Chicago, where he majored in English and Political Science. Mr. Williams also attended the University of Memphis, where he studied journalism. He resides in Chicago, Illinois, and currently serves as the president of Pollster Media Group, Inc., a book and newspaper publishing firm headquartered in Chicago.